Ac
Honoi

"*Honoring the Generations* challenges its readers to deal with the complexities of calling people to faith and developing churches in the midst of generational change, cultural adaptation, and the struggles of minority identity development. The contributors write from their experiences within their various Asian North American communities, drawing out specific insights for ministering within ANA circles, but also addressing issues that cross ethnic and cultural lines."

—Juan Francisco Martínez, Associate Provost for Diversity and International Programs, Fuller Theological Seminary

"This engaging conversation among Asian North American (ANA) ministers and professors names numerous challenges—including generational differences, cultural diversity, public engagement, assimilation, and gender inequality. The writers put their on-the-ground experiences on the table, reflect on historical elements, cultural influences, and biblical passages, and clarify what is important for ANA churches."

—Mark Lau Branson, EdD, Homer Goddard Associate Professor of Ministry of the Laity, Fuller Theological Seminary, and coauthor of *Churches, Cultures & Leadership: A Practical Theology of Congregations & Ethnicities*

"In *Honoring the Generations*, noted Asian North American theologians and pastors from varying theological traditions and cultural backgrounds honor and draw strength from disparate church experiences. The writers share the fruit of a long and sometimes arduous dialogue in hopes of inspiring a Kingdom revolution in the church that is both generative and generous for first-, second-, and third-generation ANA Christians alike."

—S. Steve Kang, Professor of Educational Ministries & Interdisciplinary Studies, Gordon-Conwell Theological Seminary, and coauthor of *Teaching the Faith, Forming the Faithful*, and *A Many-Colored Kingdom*

"The Asian North American voices in this volume have much to teach evangelicals across the spectrum who are ready to escape the western cultural captivity of the church."

—Amos Yong, J. Rodman Williams Professor of Theology, Regent University School of Divinity

"In an increasingly diverse nation, the biblical, theological, and practical insights and lessons in this must-read book will go a long way in helping congregational leaders confront the cross-cultural and cross-generational challenges of their ministry. A relevant and robust practical ecclesiology by a variety of voices that will prove to be a gift to the Christian church at large and not just to Asian North American congregations."

—Rev. Eldin Villafane, PhD, Professor of Christian Social Ethics and Founding Director of the Center for Urban Ministerial Education (CUME), Gordon-Conwell Theological Seminary

"Here in these pages are fresh lessons from Scripture, inspiring ministry stories, and an array of leadership insights to help the Asian North American church take needed next steps toward a better future."

—Russell Yee, ThM, PhD, Adjunct Professor, Fuller Theological Seminary, and author, *Worship on the Way: Exploring Asian North American Christian Experience*

"Rich in Scripture, overflowing with grace, easy to understand, respectful of complex variables, and humble about methods, this is a book for our time."

—Miriam Adeney, PhD, Associate Professor of Global and Urban Ministry, Seattle Pacific University, and author, *Kingdom without Borders: The Untold Story of Global Christianity*

"The challenges and conflicts surrounding the issues of generation, gender, leadership, evangelism, and social engagement are not unique to them, but common themes for all evangelicals in the contemporary social and cultural contexts."

—Fenggang Yang, University Faculty Scholar, Professor of Sociology and Director, Center on Religion and Chinese Society, Purdue University

"With a scarcity of such resources available, *Honoring the Generations* is a long awaited and welcome book. Connecting the significant biblical and Asian North American cultural themes such as honor and household, the authors integrate both ANA contexts and biblical principles to foster a thriving ANA ministry."

—Rev. Young Lee Hertig, PhD, Executive Director, Institute for the Study of Asian American Christianity (ISAAC)

HONORING
THE
GENERATIONS
✝
LEARNING WITH
ASIAN NORTH AMERICAN
CONGREGATIONS

M. SYDNEY PARK, SOONG-CHAN RAH,
AND **AL TIZON,** EDITORS

FOREWORD BY KEN UYEDA FONG
AFTERWORD BY BIAK MANG

JUDSON PRESS
PUBLISHERS SINCE 1824

Join our mailing list for updates and special offers.
www.judsonpress.com/mailing_list.cfm

Interior design by Beth Oberholtzer.
Cover design by Tobias Becker and Birdbox Graphic Design. www.birdboxdesign.com

Library of Congress Cataloging-in-Publication Data

Honoring the generations : learning with Asian North American congregations / M. Sydney Park, Soong-Chan Rah, and Al Tizon, editors ; foreword by Ken Uyeda Fong.
     p. cm.
    Proceedings of a conference held in May 2009 at Trinity Evangelical Divinity School, Deerfield, Ill.
    Includes bibliographical references.
    ISBN 978-0-8170-1706-4 (pbk. : alk. paper) 1. Asian American churches—North America--Congresses. 2. Intergenerational relations—North America—Congresses. I. Park, M. Sydney. II. Rah, Soong-Chan. III. Tizon, Al.
    BR563.A82.H66 2012
    277'.08308995—dc23

                    2011047856

Printed in the U.S.A.
First Edition, 2012.

CONTENTS
✝

Foreword by Ken Uyeda Fong   vii

Editors' Preface   ix

Introduction   xiii
Peter T. Cha and Al Tizon

1. Theology of the Household of God: Identity
and Function of Christ's Body in Ephesians   1
M. Sydney Park

PART ONE:
FROM GENERATION TO GENERATION

2. Intergenerational Ministry: Why Bother?   21
Mitchell Kim and David Lee

3. The Disillusioned Generation: Ecclesiology
from the Margins   39
Gideon Tsang and Soong-Chan Rah

4. Now-Generation Ministry   59
Sam S. Kim and M. Sydney Park

PART TWO:
MINISTRY ISSUES

5. Forming "Grace-Full" Pastors   81
Peter T. Cha and Greg J. Yee

6. The Way Home: Brothers and Sisters Serving Together   100
Grace Y. May and Peter K. Yi

7. Formation of Servants in God's Household 120
Nancy Sugikawa and M. Sydney Park

8. Children of Light: Following Jesus in Public Life 148
Timothy Tseng and Jonathan Wu

9. Extending Grace and Reconciliation: From
Broken Households to the Ends of the Earth 169
John E. Chung and Al Tizon

Conclusion: Moving Forward and Outward 197
Soong-Chan Rah

Afterword by Biak Mang 203

About the Contributors 205

FOREWORD
✝

Ever since I finally agreed that God was calling me to be a third-generation American Chinese pastor, I have been trying to imagine what future Asian North American (ANA) Christian churches will be like. Back in the late 1970s as I began my seminary education, I freely admitted that part of my motivation was self-serving. How could someone as Americanized as I fit comfortably in existing ANA churches, which were all immigrant-weighted and -led?

Not long after I moved to Los Angeles to finish at a different seminary, I was awarded an internship at Evergreen Baptist Church of Los Angeles, a church that was planted in 1925 to reach Japanese immigrants in East LA but that by the late 1970s was being led by a third-generation Japanese American pastor. Other Americanized Chinese young adults like me were leaving their bilingual churches, attracted not just to the English-only situation, but even more so to the emerging ethos of one of the first efforts to create a church that was a blend of different East Asian American groups.

Only a few years into living out this experiment, I sought out one of the foremost leaders of English-speaking Chinese churches in North America. A few months before, I had hardly been able to contain my excitement when I heard him preach about the desperate need for "new wineskins" in historically Chinese churches if we were ever going to reach the vast number of unsaved American Born Chinese (ABC). But after I shared about our English-only fusion of second- and third-generation Japanese and Chinese Americans, he told me that I was "thirty years too soon." He warned that the immigrant churches in America weren't ready for that model, that I would be wise to embrace the status quo, to become bilingual, and maybe even go to Hong Kong to find a trilingual wife. For now I should faithfully reach and serve their young people.

It's obvious to anyone who has bothered to track my ministry journey that I ignored that advice (in direct violation of an Asian prime directive!). By the grace of God and often by the seat of my pants, I've been privileged to be at or near the centers for reaching, equipping, and sending more Americanized Asian North Americans with "new wineskins." We still have a long, long way to go, but believe me: we definitely aren't stuck on the status quo anymore.

However, in deference to that concerned ANA church leader, it actually did take thirty years until this remarkable resource emerged—a volume that I wholeheartedly believe can finally alleviate much of the anxiety, frustration, and confusion that has been part of the varied journeys of ANA churches thus far. In *Honoring the Generations,* God's Spirit has finally provided us with a theologically calibrated and field-tested GPS that will guide us more harmoniously, more inclusively, and maybe even more rapidly to the many different places where God is leading ANA churches.

As impressed as I am with the work of the individual editors and coauthors of each essay, I am equally moved by their shared commitment to include a diversity of voices and experiences beneath Christ's all-encompassing banner of grace and unity. How this book came together is proof of how God's Spirit can fit together different generations, different genders, and different theological perspectives into the Household of God in Christ Jesus.

This superb book is not so much about *what* ANA churches should do as it is about why they should pursue a future that will bless each generation and, in the process, more clearly embrace God's coming kingdom for this world.

Rev. Dr. Ken Uyeda Fong
Evergreen Baptist Church of Los Angeles
Los Angeles, California

EDITORS' PREFACE

✝

Being the church in the world is hard enough. Add to this the complexity of a congregation comprised of people from another culture planted in foreign soil, and the difficulty is heightened. Add yet another level of complexity to this same congregation twenty to thirty years later as first and second/third generations coexist, and the difficulty can reach unmanageable heights. This book seeks to provide biblical and theological resources to help congregational leaders—particularly, but not exclusively, in the Asian North American (ANA) church—to manage these cross-cultural and cross-generational complexities.

In May 2009 more than one hundred ANA scholars and practitioners in the United States and Canada gathered together at Trinity Evangelical Divinity School in Deerfield, Illinois, for a consultation on the state of various ministries in ANA churches from a theological perspective. This book is a culmination of the insights culled from this gathering, and true to the mix of participants at the consultation, almost every chapter of this book is a collaborative effort between a scholar—one who works primarily in the academy—and a practitioner—one who works primarily in the church or a parachurch organization.

As the editors of this volume, we wholeheartedly affirm the integral relationship between theological reflection and the practice of ministry and therefore also wholeheartedly affirm the value of the scholar-practitioner tandem that was formed for each chapter. But precisely because of the multiplicity and the range of orientation of the authors (on the scholar-practitioner continuum), putting this book together was no easy task, sometimes even downright torturous! Differences between formal and informal writing styles, denominational backgrounds, ministry experiences, and theological perspectives, not to mention differing personalities, posed a formidable challenge as we sought to bring this kind of diversity together in one volume. We decided that it would be easier just to write our own books in our own voices next time!

Jesting aside, we did struggle with the temptation to make the chapters conform to our own images. The struggle intensified as we encountered perspectives and strategies that we ourselves disagreed with. We ultimately resisted, however, allowing the authors to speak for themselves. This book, therefore, represents a variety of perspectives and not a unified theology and strategy. Needless to say then, these chapters do not necessarily reflect the views of the organizers of the consultation or the editors of this book.

On behalf of all of the authors, we wish to thank the boards of the Catalyst Leadership Center and the Carl F. H. Henry Center for Theological Understanding for underwriting both the consultation and book project. Thanks also to Rebecca Irwin-Diehl and the editorial team at Judson Press for believing in this project and thereby giving Asian North American church leaders the opportunity to share their insights with the larger body of Christ.

We feel honored to have been asked by the consultation organizers to put this book together. Having our feet planted in both the academic and practical ministry worlds, we hope that the commitment to both theological reflection and effective ministry practice comes through in these pages. We believe we speak for all involved in this project when we say that it is only through theologically informed ministry and lived, ministry-soaked theology (praxis) that the church can effectively address the crucial cross-cultural and cross-generational issues of our time. Furthermore, we believe we speak for all when we say that we engage in this kind of theological praxis because we love the church in all of her diverse glory and see her potential to be God's emissary of love and justice in the world.

M. Sydney Park
Beeson Divinity School
Samford University, Birmingham, Alabama

Soong-Chan Rah
North Park Theological Seminary
North Park University, Chicago, Illinois

Al Tizon
Palmer Theological Seminary
Eastern University, Wynnewood, Pennsylvania

INTRODUCTION
✝

PETER T. CHA AND AL TIZON

During my doctoral study years, I (Peter) was also a busy church-planting pastor, making it challenging for me to spend time with my family. One evening, during our dinner, my five-year-old son suddenly blurted out, "Dad, I think you should get a new job."

Wrestling with feelings of guilt, I asked, "What kind of a job do you want me to get, Nathaniel?"

"Garbage man, Dad," came the quick reply.

Surprised and puzzled, I asked him why, and my young son explained cheerfully, "Because the garbage man works only on Wednesdays!"

Having seen that the green garbage truck comes to our street only on Wednesdays, Nathaniel must have been thinking, "Wouldn't it be wonderful if my dad had that job so that he could be home more?"

Seeing a more complete, and therefore a more accurate, picture of reality around us is a daunting task, not only for a young child, but for all of us. Shaped by one's own personal experiences and sociocultural context, each of us may see clearly certain aspects of a given reality while failing to see others. Yet in today's rapidly changing world, one's ability to see the fuller picture of what is happening is even more critical, especially for those of us who are engaged in the ministry of the gospel.

When the Catalyst Leadership Center[1] and the Carl F. H. Henry Center for Theological Understanding[2] decided to sponsor the first ever Asian North American (ANA) Consultation on Theology and

Ministry in May 2009, the primary purpose was to provide a space in which ANA ministry colleagues could collaborate to see the fuller picture of what God is doing in, through, and among ANA congregations. From its beginning in 1991, the Catalyst Leadership Center sought to reach out to and serve a wide range of Asian congregations in both Canada and the United States, and it aimed to continue this emphasis in this consultation. While a significant number of the participants came from East Asian American backgrounds, the organizers intentionally invited many participants from Southeast Asian, Filipino, and Indian congregations.

We were also very intentional about inviting participants from different regions in the United States and Canada, since ANA experiences can be strongly shaped by the particularities of each region. Furthermore, we also aimed to have a range of denominational diversity in this gathering, inviting colleagues from both conservative and mainline denominations. This rich diversity among our participants played a key role in informing our corporate reflections and conversations, enabling all of us to see the fuller picture of what God is doing in and through ANA churches.

Specifically, we had three goals and objectives for this three-day gathering. First, we desired to study the Epistle to the Ephesians together to deepen our understanding of the nature and the mission of God's church. Second, we wanted to attain a more comprehensive picture of the current experiences and practices of various ANA congregations. And finally, bringing together our insights from the *text* of God's Word and the *context* of ANA congregational ministry, we sought to engage in reflections that would integrate our theology and ministry in a deeper way.

A Consultation, Not a Conference

Most conferences are organized around the practice of listening to a few experts. The speakers present their carefully prepared materials, and the audience receives them; the interaction between the two groups is minimal. In light of the consultation's stated goals, the Catalyst board members envisioned a very different type of gathering. While there were some presentations offered by a few individuals, their main aim was to provide a framework in which group reflections and conversations could take place. Therefore, during the three days of our consultation, we spent more than half of our time in working groups or tracks that were organized around significant ministry themes, which, not incidentally, serve as the basic framework for the present volume. In each track, cofacilitated by a theologian and a ministry practitioner, ten to fifteen participants—comprised also of theologians and practitioners—consulted with one another, interacting with Scripture as well as with their respective ministry experiences.

Collaboration between Theologians and Practitioners of Ministry

The organizers of the consultation[3] decided early on that the core value that would shape all aspects of this gathering should be collaboration, a kind of rich interaction that would enable us not only to learn from one another but also to partner together in moving toward development of our own, contextualized theological framework for ANA churches. In order to facilitate such a process, the consultation gathering intentionally sought to embrace authentic collaboration by inviting both academicians and practitioners.[4]

We are both pastors and seminary professors, and as such, we have been greatly nurtured by both ecclesial and academic communities. Yet, at the same time, we have also observed over the years that these two communities rarely come together for mutual learning and partnership. We suspect that one of the main reasons is a shared underlying assumption that it is the theologian's job to produce theological works while it is the practitioner's job to find ways to apply these theological truths in their ministries. One of the consequences of such a division of labor is that theological works, developed in an isolated academic setting, can easily become detached from the life and ministry of the church, thus undermining their ability to serve and equip God's church. What might it look like if theologians and practitioners of ministry were to engage in the work of doing theological reflections collaboratively? How might the outcome of such reflections look different and further enrich the church? What potential fruit might emerge as colleagues from these two communities begin to network with one another and continue to practice a collaborative partnership in an ongoing way?

In the consultation (and in this volume), M. Sydney Park started the process of theological reflections by offering her exegetical insights on Ephesians, focusing particularly on the theme of the household of God (Eph. 2:19). Using her presentation as our starting point and our framework, the participants then met in the eight consultation tracks and engaged in the following questions: (1) What are some significant theological insights from Ephesians that can deepen our understanding of the nature and mission of the church? (2) How should these theological insights inform and guide the ANA congregations' understanding of their identity and mission given their particular social and cultural contexts? And how should they guide the church's view and practice of the particular area of ministry each track is exploring? (3) In what ways might these theological reflections transform our views of this specific ministry, and how might it contribute to overall congregational formation?

Writing Collaboratively

In order to share the various insights that emerged from the consultation, the Catalyst board team decided from the outset that the work accomplished in this consultation would culminate in the publication of a book. In doing so, we wanted the book to capture the collaborative spirit of the consultation and accurately convey the insights that emerged from corporate reflections. Therefore, during both plenary and consultation track settings, note takers carefully recorded the conversations. Then, equipped with the notes from the consultation gathering, a team of writers (a total of sixteen, two writers representing each consultation track) came together again in July 2009 to work on the overall structure of the book as well as each chapter's content. Producing a multiauthor book has many challenges and can be very time-consuming; however, given our strong commitment to collaboration, we could not consider other alternatives with any degree of seriousness.

Our collaboration covered the full range of challenges, from differences in theological perspectives to varying writing styles and everything in between. If readers expect this volume to speak with one voice, promoting unified theology and a clear strategy, they will be disappointed. But if they desire to hear a multitude of perspectives that are united only by their desire for harmonious and effective ministries between generations, they might find the insights contained in these pages to be helpful. Through this whole process, what we aimed to produce was a book that is neither abstract theology nor a practical how-to manual; rather, our goal was to develop a collaborative work that intentionally integrates rich theology and wise practice. We will let you be the final judge on whether we succeeded with the final product.

The Structure of the Book

This volume is divided into two main sections. After Park's theological treatise on the household of God based on Paul's letter to the Ephesians (chapter 1), part 1 (chapters 2–4) takes on the thorny issue of the relationship between first and second/third generations in the ANA church from three different angles. Of all the questions that impact immigrant churches, the relationship between the generations poses the greatest one. In many ways, the generational question informs all of the issues, tensions, and conflicts that occur in the various ministries of the immigrant church. To deal with both its theological and practical complexities is the beginning of bringing harmony between the generations and thus grounding the ministries of the church in strong, healthy, theologically informed relationships.

Part 2 (chapters 5–9) addresses some fundamental areas of church ministry. These areas—pastoral formation, women in ministry, lay leadership, public life, and global mission—are inevitably affected by the generational issue. Following a loose pattern of (1) story, (2) critical assessment, (3) biblical/theological foundation, (4) hope, and

(5) strategy, each of the chapters seeks to provide both theological and practical resources for those "in the trenches" of cross-cultural and cross-generational church ministry.

Soong-Chan Rah then caps the book with a concluding word and a charge. For the nature of such a book carries with it a privilege and a responsibility—namely, to engage in theology for the sake of the household of God and for the transformation of the world.

✦

NOTES

1. Since 1991 the Catalyst Leadership Center has aimed to serve the Asian North American Christian community by focusing on the task of mentoring, resourcing, and supporting its leaders. Over the years, the Center sponsored numerous pastors' conferences and mentorship programs, as well as facilitated the publication of *Growing Healthy Asian American Churches* (Downers Grove, IL: InterVarsity, 2006).

2. The Henry Center, located in Trinity Evangelical Divinity School, aims to bring together ministers, professionals, and theologians to work collaboratively in addressing some critical kingdom issues that face today's church and world. (Please visit henrycenter.org for more information.)

3. The organizers of this event consisted of the board members of the Catalyst Leadership Center—Peter Cha, associate professor of pastoral theology at Trinity Evangelical Divinity School; Paul Kim, pastor of the Open Door Presbyterian Church in Herndon, Virginia; Soong-Chan Rah, associate professor of evangelism at North Park Theological Seminary; Nancy Sugikawa, associate pastor of the Lighthouse Christian Church in Bellevue, Washington; Jonathan Wu, executive pastor of the Evergreen Baptist Church of Los Angeles in Rosemead, California; Greg Yee, associate superintendent of the Pacific Southwest Conference of the Evangelical Covenant Church, and Linda Cannell, academic dean of North Park Theological Seminary.

4. Among the participants, 51 were pastors, 24 served in parachurch organizations, 25 were seminary faculty members and 7 were full-time seminary students. Also, 28 participants were women.

CHAPTER 1

✝

Theology of the Household of God

Identity and Function of Christ's Body in Ephesians

M. SYDNEY PARK

When I received the invitation to participate as a coleader in one of the tracks in this consultation, I considered it as an opportunity to revisit a ministry context from my past. And most certainly in the past several months, I have not only asked, "What is the household of God?" but more importantly, from my experience with Asian North American (ANA) churches, "Can I call our churches 'households of God'?" Recognizing that my experience is not necessarily the same as that of others, I have a difficult time equating Korean American churches to the "household of God."

This is not to say that my experience was entirely negative; indeed, I had many warm and encouraging moments, and I certainly made wonderful acquaintances. My experiences with preaching and discipleship are some of my most treasured memories. Yet I remain uncertain whether these churches were in their identity and function "households of God." They functioned more as a social oasis for Korean immigrants. Ethics were determined by cultural and social ethos rather than Scripture; leadership appointments were most definitely not determined by knowledge of Scripture or piety. Yet some of the worship services were the most poignant I

1

have experienced as a Christian, and some, if not all, demonstrated faith that would receive commendation even from the author of Hebrews. These were, and indeed are, glimmers of hope in the midst of an all-too-imperfect situation. They provide the occasion for further examination, evaluation, and dialogue on how the ANA church can move forward to embrace and embody the identity as the "household of God."

But first things first: What exactly is the household of God? Some general comments are in order. The phrase or the concept "household of God" appears in the Gospels, some Pauline epistles, 1 Peter, and Hebrews as a loose designation for the community of God.[1] While the concept is common in the New Testament, it is not without Old Testament precedence. In the Septuagint, the term *oikos* can mean "family" or "race" (Gen. 7:1); it can also describe a holy place (Gen. 28:17,19,22) or temple (1 Chron. 17:4ff.). The fact that "house of God" refers to a temple structure is confirmed by Jesus in Mark 11:17[2] as he cites Isaiah 56:7 (and Jer. 7:11): "Is it not written, 'My house shall be called a house of prayer for all the nations'? But you have made it a den of robbers"[3] (ESV).

The notion that God's temple is called the "house of God" is highly significant for the New Testament since the Christian community itself is called "house of God."[4] This connection between "house of God" and God's temple, as we will see, becomes explicit in Ephesians 2. But Jesus' understanding of the temple as his Father's house becomes even more interesting in John 2 where the physical temple structure is explicitly identified as Jesus' body: "'Destroy this temple, and in three days I will raise it up.' The Jews then said, 'It has taken forty-six years to build this temple, and will you raise it up in three days?' But he was speaking about the temple of his body" (vv. 19-21, ESV).

The understanding of Jesus' body as the temple or "house of God" becomes explicit in Ephesians 4:15-16 where the people of God are described as Christ's body. There the "house of God" as a temple necessarily holds connotations of worship, prayer, service, sacrifice, and communion with God or God's presence. And the context of Jesus' sacrifice on the cross adds another layer of significance. The "house of God" is not a physical construction, but a living organism composed of people who are now "members" through Christ's self-sacrifice. And according to Hebrews 10:14, Christ's atonement is perfect for all time. Thus, the "house of God" as a temple of God is no longer determined by sequential sacrifice. The identity and the function of "house of God" are now defined primarily through the completeness of Christ's work on the cross. This preliminary definition of "household of God" will develop in various ways, as we consider the following three aspects: (1) the household of saving grace: the foundation; (2) the household of unity: the core nature; and (3) the household of healthy practices and ethics: the function.

The Household of Saving Grace: The Foundation

We begin with what may seem all too familiar and rudimentary: "saved by grace."[5] This simple phrase encapsulates Paul's understanding of the gospel throughout his letters. Here in his letter to the Ephesians, he speaks primarily to Gentile Christians. After an unusually lengthy section on the spiritual blessings in Christ (1:3-14) and prayer for the Ephesians (1:15-23), Paul reminds the Gentile Christians of this simple truth concerning their salvation in 2:8: "For by grace you are those saved through faith. And this [is] not from your own efforts, [but is] a gift of God."

For us in the twenty-first century, the radical nature of this statement has been all but forgotten. While it is one of the core doctrinal beliefs for evangelicals, its cultural and theological offensiveness is often neglected; and while it may be preached in the pulpit, it rarely permeates the daily routine of work, family, or even church. But in the first century, this simple claim "saved by grace" was culturally and theologically offensive for both Jews and Jewish Christians.

Paul claims that membership in the household of God, or "salvation," is not defined by Law observance or ethnic heritage, but exclusively on the redeeming work of Jesus Christ on the cross.[6] Many Israelites of the time considered these two aspects—ethnic heritage (culture) and Law observance (theology)—to be one and the same.

Abraham and his children are culled out from all other surrounding cultures to be God's people and entrusted with the Law as evidence of this salvific relationship (see Exod. 19:5-6). So, they reasoned, those who qualify for salvation are the descendants of Abraham and those who observe the Law. Thus, they believed salvation was exclusive, culturally bound to one specific people group. But note also that this cultural exclusion or racial discrimination was determined not by skin color or even ethnicity, but theology. To be an Israelite was to be a member of the only people group on earth called to be "people of God." And Law observance further segregated Israel from all other people.

We can therefore perceive the offensiveness of John the Baptist's message to the Pharisees and Sadducees in Matthew 3:7-10 and more broadly to a Jewish crowd in Luke 3:7-9: "You brood of vipers! Who warned you to flee from the wrath to come? Then bear the fruit worthy of repentance and do not think to say to yourselves: 'We have Abraham as father.' For I say to you that God is able from these stones to raise children of Abraham." For people who understood their salvation to be anchored on paternal heritage and Law observance, John's critique was not only repugnant but ludicrous.

John's radical preaching to the Jews served as an appropriate introduction to Jesus' ministry. Although Jesus' ministry was primarily directed to the Jews, two factors allude to the possibility that salvation was not to be defined by ethnicity or law observance: (1) positive reception of the "unclean" and Gentiles, and (2) critique against Jewish leadership. And indeed, the boundary-breaking nature of the gospel becomes explicit for Peter in Acts 10 when he is exhorted, "What God has cleansed, you should not call common" (v. 15). Through the salvation of Cornelius and his household, Peter learns that "God shows no partiality, but in every nation anyone who fears him and does what is right is acceptable to him" (vv. 34-35, ESV). Peter's experience with Cornelius serves as the key argument for Gentile inclusion apart from Law observance at the Jerusalem Council in Acts 15:7-11: neither Jew nor Gentile is saved by law observance, but both are saved by grace. The early church did not fully realize this radical nature of the gospel until the Jerusa-

lem Council, which occurred at least a decade after the first Easter
(c. 44 CE). Paul's simple claim "saved by grace" in Ephesians 2:8
was culturally and theologically radical.[7] And indeed, in spite of
resistance to Gentile inclusion apart from law observance, Paul in-
sists in Romans 4:16-17 that all who live by faith are descendants of
Abraham. Then the radical claim is undoubtedly the fulfillment of
God's promise to Abraham in Genesis 17:5: "I have made you the
father of many nations."

Is this message "saved by grace" still controversial for twenty-
first-century believers? More specifically, is this message controversial for ANA Christians? What are the implications of "saved by
grace" for a culture driven by strong work ethics where confidence
and identity of the individual are anchored on achievement and success? Is membership in God's household based on accomplishment
or penitent recognition of our spiritual bankruptcy—that apart from
grace salvation is not possible? And if we are to account for Paul's
reasoning why we are saved by grace and not by works, "so that
no one should boast" (Eph. 2:9), can confidence and identity continue to be founded on works? If there is no demarcation between
"clean" and "unclean" and all are "unclean," only made clean by
God's grace, how should we perceive ourselves and others within
and without the church? If ethnic boundaries of Jew and Gentile are
irrelevant in Christ, what are the implications for ANA churches?
"Saved by grace," a simple statement that has lost its original offensiveness, needs to be reasserted as the foundation for the church
with all its radical implications.

At this point, I want to add another layer to the theological statement "saved by grace." This phrase occurs at the end of Ephesians
2:1-10 where Paul reminds the Gentiles precisely what salvation
means in terms of lifestyle, mind-set, and identity. This passage is
dominated by several antithetical themes: life prior to salvation,
life after salvation; life of death, life of resurrection from the dead;
salvation not by works but grace, saved not by works but saved
for works. If the antithesis running throughout the passage serves
to radically distinguish life prior to salvation from life after salvation, then is there also a distinction between the perception of works

prior to salvation and after salvation? Works serving as the basis for boasting is negated in salvation based on the fact that we are "saved by grace." But works are a necessary result of salvation. What is the categorical difference between the two?

Perhaps 2:9 provides the answer: works are not the basis of our confidence in salvation. Our identity and self-worth are exclusively anchored in God's saving activity. And on the basis of this firm foundation, we "walk" in good works—works are the product and not the source of our identity in Christ. And if the antithetical parallels of the passage are to be taken seriously, perhaps the following can be applied to works: to perceive works as the foundation of our identity and self-esteem is to revert back to a mind-set prior to salvation. For an Asian mind-set and ethos driven by strong work ethics, how significant is the proper understanding of works? Does this cultural ethos, oftentimes perceived as a virtue, require reassessment? And if changing a cultural mind-set ossified through countless generations is a challenge, then how does Paul's conversion from righteousness by works to that of God (Phil. 3:2-9) provide hope?

The Household of Unity: The Core Nature

In Ephesians 2:11-22, Paul explores the implication of "saved by grace" with respect to Jew-Gentile relations. Thus, the dominant theme in this passage is racial reconciliation. However, the theology contained within cannot be exclusively limited to racial reconciliation but has wider implications. For Paul, the historic enmity between Jew and Gentile is now resolved in the cross:

> But now in Christ you who once were far off have been brought near in the blood of Christ. For he is our peace, who has made us both one, and has broken down the dividing wall of hostility, by abolishing in his flesh the law of commandments and ordinances, that he might create in himself one new man in place of the two, so making peace, and might reconcile us both to God in one body through the cross, thereby bringing the hostility to an end. (vv. 13-16)

What is highly significant here is that Paul explores reconciliation between humans first, before he deals with reconciliation between God and humanity (v. 18). While undoubtedly the primary theological implication of the cross is vertical reconciliation (God-humanity), here Paul emphasizes the horizontal reconciliation (humanity-humanity). Where there were two, now there is one; where there was enmity, now there is peace. The Gentile is no longer excluded but is an equal member with Jews in the same household of God (v. 19). The long-standing historic enmity is now resolved not because either sought out the other or asked for forgiveness, but because hostility is resolved based on the cross alone.

The notions of reconciliation, unity, and peace describe the household of God. This was the purpose of the cross. It is not simply the case of "me and my" reconciliation with God, for the cross necessarily holds communal implications. A church that does not demonstrate reconciliation, unity, and peace has not fully grasped the theological significance of the cross. We forgive and reconcile not because the offender has finally repented or even asked for forgiveness; we seek out unity within the body not because we all agree theologically, politically, or even culturally. We strive for peace not because we have nonconfrontational or repressive personalities— we live in reconciliation, unity, and peace *because* these have been accomplished in the cross.

To what extent do these elements of reconciliation, unity, and peace describe our churches? If I am saved by grace and not by merit, how can I continue to view others by merit? Or does salvation by grace mandate not only receiving grace, but extending grace to others? And if reconciliation with God is provided through the cross and the same cross is the source of reconciliation with one another, when there is no evidence of reconciliation among one another, how can there be reconciliation with God? How does this affect internal relations of the church? How does this affect intergenerational issues?

But if we are to seek out reconciliation, unity, and peace, another factor needs to be explored. At the end of this passage, Paul calls this household of God, now created by the cross, "a holy temple in the Lord" (Eph. 2:21). The temple is symbolically rich—it is the dwelling place of God with the provision of atonement so that there might be unity between God and his people. According to Paul, the household of God is now that temple; humanity now has access to the Father (v. 18) and is now to be a dwelling place of God (vv. 21-22). And this "temple" is a corporate entity in which all the members of the household of God are "joined together and grow[s] into a holy temple" (v. 21).

Being Built Up in the Household

In Ephesians 2:20-22, the metaphor of building is heavily emphasized and connects well with the notion of "household of God" in 2:19: "having been built" (v. 20), "the whole building" (v. 21), "you are being built" (v. 22), and "dwelling place" (v. 22). This new community is a structure that is "being joined or fitted together" (v. 21). The word *harmologeō* with the prefix *syn* means "to join or pile together," and in the context of the first-century construction process, the absence of mortar required each stone to be cut and tailored to fit with another.[8] *Synharmologeō* is immediately followed by the verb "to grow" and conveys an ongoing process. Thus, the process of being "fitted together" is coherent with the process of growth, and the process of growth is *continual*. Each stone in the entire structure, being cut and fashioned to fit the other, seems to indicate that while reconciliation is effectively accomplished at the cross, the process of growing into a "dwelling place of God" requires continual accommodation of each other.[9]

It is often said that the problem with the church is not God, but God's people. Living together, even for Christians, is more often than not frustrating and painful. How does the interpretation of Ephesians 2:21 affect our perspective on internal disputes? Are some of the challenges we face within the church simply "growing pains"? Does the notion that growth is a continual process exasperate or provide an eschatological perspective on these "difficulties"—and why? And in this process of being cut to fit one another, growing continually into a temple, how does the knowledge that God is the active agent in this building process (v. 22) provide comfort and confidence?

Unity and Diversity in the Household

Paul continues to develop this theme of unity within the household of God in Ephesians 4. Here the metaphor for "building" already broached in chapter 2 continues and incorporates different nuances necessary for the household of God. In verses 1-2, Paul enumerates certain dispositions coherent to the household of God: humility, meekness, patience, and endurance of one another with love. These character traits are indispensable in the effort to maintain unity of the Spirit (v. 3), a unity that takes place through peace. The endeavor to maintain unity and peace is not merely human activity, but the activity of the Holy Spirit.[10] There is no division between divine and human activity; but provision of unity through the Holy Spirit necessarily implies coherent human obedience to maintain this gift. Further, if the church is indeed the product of divine activity, then it is without exception coherent to God who calls the church to faith in him. Just as there is unity within the Godhead, there is unity within the body. The entirety of verses 4-6 lays emphasis on the oneness of God. Thus, the exhortation to maintain unity in verses 2-3 is anchored in the theological claim that unity is coherent to the Trinitarian God.[11]

But unity within the household of God does not preclude diversity of gifts. Paul claims that "building up" or "edification" of the church also needs "equipping" or "training" of the saints (Eph. 4:12). Indeed, for Paul, the result of Christ's ascent is "giving gifts to all" (v. 8),[12] and these gifts are listed in verse 11 as apostles, prophets, evangelists, pastors, and teachers. All these gifts are to be used for the work of the ministry, which "builds up" Christ's body. And this process of "building up" has a certain eschatological goal: "until all should attain unto the unity of faith and the knowledge of the Son of God, unto complete/mature humanity, unto the measure of the stature of the fullness of Christ" (v. 13). There is one primary goal of all these gifts—it is not for one, but for all to strive toward a certain goal.[13] The eschatological tone is palpable. And this "goal" is described in three dimensions.

First, the various gifts build up the church so that there is unity of faith and unity in the knowledge of Jesus Christ. Second, the same gifts also are employed to lead the church to maturity. More precisely, the phrase is "mature person" and best refers to spiritual/ethical maturity of believers, in contrast to the "spiritual infants" mentioned in Ephesians 4:14. Third and finally, the end goal of "building up" the church is to attain to the fullness of Christ. All three are part and parcel of one primary goal: maturity in Christ. And this maturity is set in opposition to what Paul defines as spiritual immaturity in verse 14: "being tossed to and fro and carried by every wind of doctrine, by the cunning of others, by their craftiness in deceitful wiles." Paul returns to the theme of unity in verse 15 with another metaphor for the church; here it is not a building construction, but a growing organism: Christ is the head (v. 15) while the church is his body (v. 16). And in this body, while all parts of the body are ultimately subject to the head, each is seamlessly joined together; yet each part has its own function and must operate properly so that the entire body grows in love.

If the household of God is a construction currently in the process of growth, then naturally, growth implies maturity. But in Ephesians, maturity is not defined temporally (age) nor by numerical growth. An organic relationship exists between the notions of unity and maturity. Maturity of the household of God can occur only as unity is demonstrated (a) toward the Godhead and the faith and (b) toward each member in the household of God. Thus, it is critical to determine whether a church is theologically coherent to the one triune God. If God is one, then the church as God's creation must also necessarily be "one." How does this theological rationale, the oneness of God, differ from culturally or socially motivated rationale for unity? To what extent is the concern for unity in the ANA church the reflection of the one triune God, and to what degree might it be simply the consequence of common Asian identity vis-à-vis the Euro-American, African American, and Hispanic cultures?

Paul further defines maturity of the household of God as "the measure of the stature of the fullness of Christ" (Eph. 4:13). In short, it is "the spiritual maturity represented by Christ's completeness."[14] Christ therefore becomes the standard for maturity of the church. To this end, the various gifts are employed so that all saints might reach this maturity through unity of faith and knowledge of the Son of God (v. 13). Spiritual immaturity is reflected by lack of discernment with respect to seductive and deceitful doctrine or "teaching"—rooted, we can assume, in a lack of knowledge about Jesus. So, for Paul, maturity of the household of God is dependent on the teaching component of the church. How central is the concern to teach correct doctrine/theology in the ANA church? To what extent is the teaching function of the church the key ingredient for spiritual maturity, that is, unity?

Growth is the tangible result of the first two components: the oneness of God and correct teaching about the fullness of Christ. If these prerequisites of maturity are in place, then the household of God grows as one body. Each part, albeit with a separate function, is connected to the whole. And as each part functions, the entire body grows. Theology is, therefore, organically tied to spiritual maturity and unity within the household of God. This is what we claim to believe, but are we acting out of that knowledge and belief?

How often is theology divorced from praxis in the church? And how should we combat such tendencies? How does the organic nature of theology and praxis help to reevaluate our approach to ministry? How often do we measure the maturity of the church by the criterion of unity? To what extent does the concept of unity operative in our churches celebrate diversity of gifts? How does the use of these diverse gifts engender further unity?

The Household of Healthy Practices and Ethics: The Function

Ethical instructions in Ephesians are not limited to one section but are sown throughout the letter. But perhaps the summary statement for all of the ethical exhortations is found in 5:1: "Therefore be imitators of God, as beloved children." The call to be imitators of God is found only here in the New Testament. Elsewhere Paul provides Christ as the model for imitation (Phil. 2:5-11) and his own life patterned after Christ (1 Cor. 4:16-17; 11:1; Phil. 3:17). And as unique as the call to be imitators of God might be, the example of Christ in 5:2 further expounds precisely what Paul means: to imitate God is to love self-sacrificially as Christ sacrificed himself for us. Both the rejection of various sinful behaviors (4:25-31; 5:3) and the commendation of appropriate behavior (4:2,3,25-32) are determined by the model of Jesus Christ's self-sacrificial love.

Ephesians 5:21 serves as the conclusion to these exhortations: "Be subject (or 'submit') to one another out of reverence for Christ." This reverence is not respect separate from submission; rather, proper reverence for Christ mandates submission.[15] The motivating reason for mutual submission within the household of God is not respect for any individual or even based on emotions, but reverence for Christ. We submit to one another *because* we submit to Christ. Again, ethics or praxis for the household of God is based on theology. Indeed, culturally or socially derived principles are not primary as the motivating rationale for ethics in the church.

How often does the ANA church promote ethics based on humanitarian principles or cultural norms? If cultural or social norms serve as the basis for ethics, then how does it cohere with "saved by grace"? How does the teaching component affect ethics—that is, does building up the knowledge of the Son of God influence our ethics in view of Ephesians 5:2 and 5:21? To what degree is "submission to one another" the apt description of the church's mind-set? If we are "saved by grace," how is it possible to walk in disunity with Christ's model of self-sacrifice?

The final summation for ethics in Ephesians 5:21 segues to further instructions for the individual family unit called "household codes." Here we will concentrate on the first two sets of relationships: wife-husband and children-parents. Both relationships are highly relevant for ANA churches. Let me begin with the cultural background of first-century Greco-Roman and Jewish culture.

In the first century (as well as centuries before and after), the relationship with respect to both male-female and child-parent relationships is hierarchical and patriarchal. This is a simple fact. In both cultures, women were not equal but were inferior to men. While modern-day studies on gender relations in antiquity indicate an elevated view of women in certain cultures (Roman and Jewish) at certain times, the positive view of women in antiquity is by no means the normative view. With respect to children, in both cultures, the father had absolute authority over his children. In Israel the father had the authority to stone a rebellious son (Deut. 21:18-21) and sell his daughter into slavery (Exod. 21:7); and physical discipline was an appropriate method of teaching (Prov. 13:24; 22:15). In the Greek culture, the father's authority was similar to that of a king over his subjects.[16] Roman culture increased the severity of the Greek's paternal authority so that the father's authority over the son's was lifelong.[17] In what way are the household codes in Ephesians 5:22–6:4 different from the hierarchy and patriarchy of gender and child-parent relations in Jewish antiquity, Greco-Roman culture, and Hellenistic Judaism? Are the household codes a concession to the concurrent cultural-social values? Several features suggest otherwise.

Husbands and Wives

The marital relationship is set within the theological parameters of Christ's love for the church (Eph. 5:23). The wife's submission is likened to the church's submission to Christ. But further, the husband's behavior is also modified by Christ's model: as Christ loved the church self-sacrificially, the husband must also love his wife self-sacrificially. The relationship is not a simple recapitulation of the wider cultural perspective but is theologically constructed by the example of Christ. In that the responsibilities of both are innately linked to the model of Christ, the operative mind-set in the relationship is that of self-sacrifice. The key factor in submission is that the concern for and of the other outweighs the concern for and of the self. And love as modeled by Christ is self-sacrificing.

Moreover, while the exhortation to the wife is relatively short, the one for the husband is extensive. The husband's love for the wife is likened to Christ's concerns for the church: sanctification, purification, and holiness. Christ's concern for the church is comprehensive and holistic; thus, the husband's love for his wife is exhorted to be similar. Given the parallel between the marital relationship and that of Christ and the church, several questions can be posed. Can the church submit to Christ apart from his self-sacrifice? Is Christ the head of the church apart from his saving work on the cross?

Philippians 2:6-11 states that *because* Christ humbled himself, God exalted him in the highest and gave him the name above all names. Submission of all in heaven, on earth, and under the earth is based on his humility, obedience, and self-sacrifice. Apart from self-sacrificial love, does the husband have authority? Does the wife's submission to the husband extend to a general principle of submission of women to men? In what way does the exhortation for the wife's submission relate to mutual submission in 5:21? Is the wife called to submit based on her inferiority? Is the call to submit for the purpose of her oppression? Does the exhortation for the wife's submission to her husband preclude women from leadership in the church?

Parents and Children

With respect to the child-parent relationship, the exhortation draws upon the fifth commandment, "Honor your father and mother." And the modifying phrase, "so that it may be well with you and that you may live long on earth" in 6:3, is a citation of Deuteronomy 5:16, but a similar phrase is also found in Exodus 20:12. The command to honor the parents is not based on whether the parents are worthy of such honor; nor is it based on the fact that they "gave life" to the children. Rather, the theological reasoning is based on the benefits to the children. The blessings of a good and long life are the benefits of honoring the parents.

Conversely, a parents' responsibility is outlined uniquely in Ephesians 6:4. According to H. W. Hoehner, the prohibitive command "Make it a practice not to anger your children" possibly suggests that fathers should not constantly nag or demean their children, for such behavior will naturally lead to resentment.[18] Instead, fathers are exhorted with the responsibility of "training and admonition of the Lord." They are to "nurture" or "rear up" their children in the education and gentle admonition (rather than sharp command) that is Christocentric (of the Lord).[19] The honoring of the parents is linked with the father's responsibility to teach his children.

In the Asian culture where the parent-child relationship is undoubtedly hierarchical and stoical, how can this exhortation be embraced? Is the exhortation to both child and parent simply a mirrored reflection of Asian culture? How does the theological motivation of "blessing" (good and long life) change our perspective on the fifth command? How well have Asian Christian fathers and mothers faithfully upheld their responsibilities by "nurturing" their children in a Christocentric manner? If reconciliation is accomplished at the cross, is reconciliation necessary between generations?

Conclusion

As we draw to a close, I will not reiterate the various points made above. But it seems reasonable to say that there is enough in Paul's letter to the Ephesians to provide a certain shape to our understanding of what it means to be the "household of God." Simultaneously, the theology of the household of God also gives us ample pause for careful thought as we look forward and consider the changes that might be necessary. I leave the precise details of growth, yes, to each individual track in this consultation, but more fundamentally to each ANA congregation. However, I do want to end by recalling the "glimmers of hope" I mentioned in the beginning.

Paul says in Philippians 1:3-6: "I thank my God in all my remembrance of you, always in every prayer of mine for you all making my prayer with joy, because of your partnership in the gospel from the first day until now. And I am sure of this, that he who began a good work in you will bring it to completion at the day of Jesus Christ" (ESV). If we fall short now, we can look forward with hope, because it is God who has begun the work in ANA churches, and he will bring it to completion. It is as S. C. Barton notes on the biblical understanding of family: "It will . . . be something to do with hope, the overcoming of sin, oppression and despair, and growth toward full humanity."[20]

Each of us here, in the midst of all our inadequacy, can have hope, because it is God who completes the work. Similarly, we can look at the current situation of ANA churches and have hope, because God completes the work he has begun. What we are now is not what we will be in ten or twenty years, not merely because it is the natural course of things to change, but because God completes what he has begun. Amen.

✦
NOTES

1. The phrase "household of God" is one of many figurative descriptions of the church in the New Testament. See Paul Minear, *Images of the Church in the New Testament* (Philadelphia: Westminster, 1977), for a comprehensive list.

2. The parallel passages in the other Gospels are Matthew 21:13; Luke 19:46; and John 2:16.

3. All translations are mine unless stated otherwise.

4. Otto Michel, "*oikos*," *TDNT* 5 (1967): 121.

5. One of the best modern-day treatments on the subject of grace is Miroslav Volf, *Free of Charge: Giving and Forgiving in a Culture Stripped of Grace* (Grand Rapids: Zondervan, 2005). Differences notwithstanding, Volf's understanding of grace as the paradigm for Christian identity and function excels as he interacts with Scripture, theology, history, and culture.

6. See also Hebrews 11:1-40 for a list of those who received commendation "by faith," and Romans 4:1-25.

7. For biblical consistency, see also Romans 4 and Hebrews 2:4; 11.

8. The construction process described in Ephesians 2:21 coheres with the prescription in 1 Kings 6:7.

9. See Richard N. Longenecker, "Paul's Vision of the Church and Community Formation," in *Community Formation in the Early Church and in the Church Today*, ed. R. N. Longenecker (Peabody, MA: Hendrickson, 2002), 73–88.

10. Andrew T. Lincoln, *Ephesians*, vol. 42 of Word Biblical Commentary (Dallas: Word, 1990), 237.

11. While the issue of unity in this paper specifically deals with unity within individual churches, the same concern for unity also requires the universal

perspective spanning denominational boundaries. For an insightful assessment of the issues, see Carl E. Braaten and Robert W. Jenson, eds., *In One Body through the Cross* (Grand Rapids: Eerdmans, 2003).

12. Ibid., 265.

13. Harold W. Hoehner, *Ephesians: An Exegetical Commentary* (Grand Rapids: Baker Academic, 2002), 552.

14. Ibid., 557.

15. Ibid., 719.

16. Gottlob Schrenk, *"patēr,"* TDNT 5 (1968): 949.

17. Jane F. Gardner, *Family and Familia in Roman Law and Life* (Oxford: Clarendon, 1998), 1–4, 117–26, 270–72.

18. Hoehner, *Ephesians*, 796.

19. Ibid. Hoehner prefers the subjective genitive, "the training and admonition that come from the Lord." But the objective genitive (teaching about the Lord) is also possible.

20. Stephen C. Barton, *Life Together: Family, Sexuality and Community in the New Testament and Today* (Edinburgh: T&T Clark, 2001), 40.

PART ONE

✝

FROM GENERATION TO GENERATION

CHAPTER 2

✝

Intergenerational Ministry

Why Bother?

MITCHELL KIM AND DAVID LEE

For eight years Pastor Mark's church had envisioned and worked to develop an operationally and financially independent English-speaking congregation in the context of an immigrant church in order to reach the many unreached Asian North Americans (ANA) in their area. The governing board had agreed to this goal in 2002, and in 2009 the English ministry (EM) was blossoming. The congregation was growing in size, and a number of young families had recently joined the church. However, with financial and operational independence clearly on the horizon, the church governing board (led by the Korean immigrant ministry) resolved that in the future the EM should remain as a subministry within the wider church. They would have no formal voice in leadership or the ongoing future of the church. Deeply discouraged and frustrated, they did not know what to do.

This story captures some of the unique challenges of intergenerational ministry within an immigrant church. The challenges in such ministries are multiplied by barriers of language and culture between the first and second generations. What should be the proper response by the EM? The most expedient answer might be to leave the church immediately with the group that had developed over the years. While the EM might flourish by striking out on its own, could such a move at that time miss out on an aspect of God's blessing in such a situation? How does God desire to release the *blessing* of the parents' generation to multiply and extend the next generation and accomplish the work of God's *kingdom*? The challenges of intergenerational ministry threaten to sever the natural connection between blessing, multiplication, and God's kingdom. In this chapter, we will seek to articulate biblical principles to undergird the outworking of practices in the often messy process of building churches across cultural and generational divides.

To explore this matrix of blessing, multiplication, and God's kingdom, this chapter will first anchor itself in Genesis 1:26-28. In this passage, God blesses Adam and Eve, and this blessing propels them to multiply and fill the earth with children in God's image (cf. Gen. 5:1-3) who will continue the work of God's kingdom. From Creation, God intended to release a divine blessing through parents to multiply children and extend God's kingdom. However, sin inevitably complicates the process of passing this blessing between generations, as evident with Noah in Genesis 9:18-29. The problem of sin, of course, is ultimately satisfied through the climactic work of Christ on the cross, which enables the rapid expansion of the church in Acts. This expansion of the church is painted, we will see, from the palette of Genesis 1:28. In this manner, we will see how God has designed his blessing to be passed from generation to generation throughout the story of the Bible.[1] On the basis of this biblical trajectory of Genesis 1:28, we hope to stir the imagination about what God could do in the intergenerational ministries of our churches.

Biblical-Theological Analysis

The Purpose of Family Is Mission (Genesis 1:26-28)

In Genesis 1:26-28, God blesses Adam and Eve, culminating in the call for multiplication: "Be fruitful and multiply and fill the earth" (ESV). This call is connected to the multiplying or extending of God's image. Adam and Eve were to multiply "images of God" that would represent God's presence and rule to the ends of the earth. This rule does not dominate or exploit for selfish gain but rather stewards creation so that it might flourish fully (see Gen. 2:15). Consequently, the call to multiply images of God is a call to extend the kingdom of God to the ends of the earth, and the divine blessing empowers and enables this multiplication. In this manner, the call to procreation is a call to extend God's kingdom through the multiplication of images of God.

What is an "image of God"? "Image" is translated in the Septuagint as *eikōn*, from which we get the English word *icon*. Today icons are ubiquitous, especially on our computer desktops. An icon itself is a very small picture file, approximately 60 kilobytes in size. However, clicking on the icon accesses the numerous and powerful resources of the program that it represents. Though the icon itself is not much, it brings about all the power of this program. In a similar manner, we are icons (images) of God. We may not seem like much, but we are representatives who bring in the presence of the powerful God whom we image in the world.[2] Images of God represent and extend God's rule to the ends of the earth. They are not only to rule over the animals but also over the forces of evil in the world.[3] Therefore, images of God must be multiplied to fill the earth so that "the earth will be filled with the knowledge of the glory of the LORD" (Hab. 2:14).[4] Therefore, the call to multiply images of God (i.e., to bear children and form families) can be understood as the foundational call for mission.

Consequently, the purpose of family is mission. As we raise up our children and the young people in our churches, we are called to form in them images of God who represent God's rule to the ends of the earth. This command is preceded by a blessing (Gen. 1:28) so that God's blessing empowers Adam and Eve to be fruitful and multiply and fill the earth. Similarly throughout the Bible, it is always God's blessing that empowers us for mission (Ps. 67; Matt. 28:18-20).

God's blessing, which empowers mission, is expressed through parents. In Genesis 1:28, God blesses the first parents, Adam and Eve, and they are blessed to fill the earth with images of God. While it is clearly God who blesses (see, e.g., Gen. 9:1; 12:2-3; 22:17), God's blessing is passed on through the human agency of the parents. We can see a powerful example of this in Genesis 49. Jacob blesses each of his twelve sons, the tribes of Israel (Gen. 49:1-28), and this blessing is worked out through the subsequent generations in the unfolding of the story of the Bible. God has designed his blessing to be passed on from one generation to the other.

In a church context, the second generation thrives as a result of the blessing of the first generation, and the first generation has a God-given responsibility to pass on that blessing to the next. Consequently, those who serve with the second generation in a church must work hard not only to reach their own generation but also to help the first generation release that blessing for their young people. God has given parents a spiritual authority that can bring tremendous blessing on the next generation, especially when released in a context of loving training and instruction. Paul reminds us that the command to honor our father and mother is "the first commandment with a promise" (Eph. 6:1-3; cf. Exod. 20:12). God's promise and blessing are realized when we as the next generation walk in a way that honors the first generation, regardless of their shortcomings. Similarly, God's purposes through the first generation are fully realized as God's blessing is passed on to the next generation.

How can we practically honor the first generation? We must not only lead and bless those below us but also those whom God has placed above us (cf. Rom. 13:1-7; 1 Pet. 2:13-17).[5] In the intergenerational church context, we must not only focus on leading our spiritual children but also our spiritual parents, helping them see how God has entrusted them with a blessing to be released to raise up powerful images of God to extend God's reign in the world. This understanding can be unlocked only when bridges of relationship are established. The second generation must earn trust from the first generation to receive their blessing; the first generation must exercise courage to release God's work in the next generation. When parents, whether spiritual or biological, understand the God-given blessing they can unlock for their children, great power is released.

This is the creation ideal—a first generation that willingly, even eagerly, blesses the next generation, thereby unlocking God's power in the lives of their children and grandchildren. But as both families of birth and of faith know, the dynamics of nurture and honor and blessing are rarely so ideal. The Genesis account provides another episode that highlights how God's blessing is extended even through flawed families.

Blessing through Flawed Families (Genesis 9:18-29)

So, how does the blessing of Genesis 1:28 get worked out in a fallen world? Sin enters the world in Genesis 3 and inaugurates a downward spiral of brokenness in the world in Genesis 4–11. However, God's blessing remains, and representatives of God created in his image continue to be multiplied on the earth (Gen. 5). After the flood, Noah is also called to "be fruitful and multiply and fill the earth" (Gen. 9:1,7; cf. Gen. 1:28). The specter of sin, though, has not been fully washed away by the flood. Noah gets drunk with the fruit of his vineyard and lies naked in his tent. Instead of honoring his father, Noah's son Ham comes in and exposes his father's nakedness, telling his brothers outside (Gen. 9:22). While nakedness was without shame in the Garden of Eden (Gen. 2:25), the exposure of nakedness after the Fall brings great shame. His brothers, Shem and Japheth, come in and cover up their father's nakedness (Gen. 9:23). As a result, Ham's son Canaan is cursed while Shem and Japheth are blessed.

Metaphorically, the second generation can easily, like Ham, expose the frailties and weaknesses of the first generation. When the first generation disappoints—when elder leaders make programming changes and ministry transitions without consulting younger members of the leadership team—the second generation can easily respond with bitterness or lash out with unhelpful criticism. The tongue is a fire, ignited by the fires of hell itself (James 3:6), and it is tempting to expose juicy details of the failures of others. At this point, the lesson of Ham and Shem is instructive: we must be careful about unnecessarily exposing the frailties of the first generation.

While we must deal with misunderstandings firmly, we must do so respectfully. The call to honor our parents is clear (Exod. 20:12).

God's blessing is extended through Noah in a context of sin. While Ham is cursed by Noah because of his failures (Gen. 9:25), God's blessing is given to Shem and Japheth in Genesis 9:26-27. God blesses and enlarges Japheth, paralleling God's earlier blessing of Noah and call to "be fruitful and multiply and fill the earth" (Gen. 9:1), but this time the blessing is extended through Noah's son.

Blessing Out of Conflict (Acts 6:1-7)

The call of Genesis 1:28 is transformed in the New Testament to focus not only on the propagation of biological children but also on spiritual children through the gospel. It takes the form of leadership development and expansion of the gospel ministry. In the book of Acts, the progress of the gospel is punctuated with reference to the language of fruitfulness and multiplication originating in Genesis 1:28:

> Acts 6:7 And the word of God continued to *increase*, and the number of the disciples *multiplied* greatly in Jerusalem, and a great many of the priests became obedient to the faith.

> Acts 12:24 But the word of God *increased and multiplied*.

> Acts 19:20 So the word of the Lord continued to *increase* and prevail mightily.

The language of Genesis 1:28 is subtly transformed to mark the growth of the word of God and not just the people of God. Just as Adam and Eve were to "increase and multiply" (Gen. 1:28), so the word of God "increased" and the disciples "multiplied greatly" (Acts 6:7).[6] While the fulfillment of Genesis 1:28 in the Old Testament primarily focused on the blood family, its fulfillment in the New Testament focuses on the family of faith (cf. Matt. 3:7-10; Mark 3:31-35; Luke 3:7-9; John 1:12-13), although it does not preclude the importance of the natural family.[7]

While God's Word must increase and bear fruit in our lives before we can expect numerical multiplication, such fruit often becomes evident and ripe through conflict. In Acts 6, the Hellenists complained to the Hebrews that their widows were being over-looked in the distribution of food. This conflict between Hellenists and Hebrews reflected a cultural tension in that day. Hellenists had assimilated to the dominant Greco-Roman culture and language.[8] In contrast, the Hebrews resisted assimilation and sought to pre-serve their Jewish heritage from "corruption" by Hellenism. In Acts 6, the Hebraic faction held the power within the church.

The similarities between this conflict and the conflict between first- and second-generation ANA Christians are striking. Although the Hellenist-Hebrew dilemma was along cultural lines,[9] the di-lemma in ANA churches runs along generational lines. However, the generational line cannot be divorced from the cultural line in the ANA context; for second/third generations have assimilated to North American culture to such a degree that the encounter be-tween first and second/third generations is nothing less than a cross-cultural one. In this light, the Hebrews can be compared to what are affectionately called "FOBs" (fresh off the boat) who reflect the immigrant culture, while the Hellenists reflect more the "Twinkies" (those yellow [Asian] on the outside yet white on the inside), second-generation ANAs who are assimilated to the wider Western culture within the church.

In the face of such conflict, the Hebrew Jews respond admirably in two ways. First, they refuse to succumb to the tyranny of the urgent; recognizing their calling to "prayer and the ministry of the word" (Acts 6:4), they do not neglect that calling to respond to the problem presented. Next, the Hebrew leadership courageously gives the Hellenists the authority to appoint deacons "full of the Spirit and wisdom" (6:3). The names of those chosen—Philip, Procho-rus, Nicanor, Timon, Parmenas, and Nicolaus from Antioch—are all Hellenistic, so it is evident that the Hebraic leadership delegated full authority to address the issue. As adequate leaders and work-ers were installed, the newly appointed deacons corrected a sharp imbalance in terms of who had a place at the table of leadership. Since the greatest growth area was in increasing the care for the Hellenistic widows, it made strategic and spiritual sense to install Hellenistic leaders. In a similar manner, the immigrant generation must continue to be faithful to their primary calling of ministering the word to immigrants, even as they are called to courageously delegate leadership to the next generation at the appropriate time.

Simultaneously, the Hellenists had spent adequate time in discipleship and character formation, so they had leaders who were "full of the Spirit and wisdom" (Acts 6:3). The need to appoint leaders did not arise out of any kind of political power play; instead, the need became evident from their mutual concern for the needy. In a similar manner, second-generation ANAs should remember that our ministry does not begin when the reins of authority are fully delegated by the first generation; it begins in the hard work of discipleship and ministry to the needy in the present. Delegation of authority is a necessary aspect of the process of maturation but is not the starting point for ministry. Indeed, unless the hard work of discipleship is taking place, then the leadership vacuums in our churches cannot be filled with trained leaders at the appropriate time.

Second-generation ANAs must take care not to blame the first generation for problems that arise from their own weaknesses and errors. We must devote our energies to developing healthy disciples, men and women "of good repute, full of the Holy Spirit and wisdom" (Acts 6:3). Only then shall we have the resources to address the problems within our ministry. At the same time, we need courageous first-generation leaders who are willing to appoint and give leadership to second-generation leaders who are adequately prepared, with mutual edification and submission.

Ultimately, the resolution of intercultural conflict in Acts 6 leads to the progress of the gospel. In Acts 6–12, the gospel spreads throughout Judea and Samaria through the ministry of the deacons appointed in Acts 6; these Hellenistic deacons, especially Philip and Stephen, become key witnesses of the gospel in the next phase of their mission (Acts 6:8–7:60; 8:4-8,26-40). The humble yet bold resolution of conflict in Acts 6 catalyzes the development of leaders for the next stage of world evangelization in Judea and Samaria.

The ANA church may be facing a similar moment of conflict as the baton of ministry is passed from one generation to another. The cultural conflict between the Hebraic and Hellenistic Jews concerned assimilation to the dominant Greek culture of that day; a similar cultural conflict faces many immigrant and second-generation ministries in ANA churches today. However, this intercultural and intergenerational conflict can, if properly addressed, propel the next generation of ANAs into the next phase of ministry effectiveness and leadership. What steps can be taken to ensure that the blessing of the first generation is passed on to the next, with the result of fruitful multiplication and kingdom growth?

Hope-Filled Imagination: Biblical Principles and Multiple Models

The history of the ANA church is littered with many stories of false starts, frustration, and pain due to generational conflict. However, we believe there is hope for a truly effective and healthy intergenerational future. Real hope can be found as we view the church through the lens of the household of God as expressed in this matrix of blessing, multiplication, and God's kingdom from Genesis 1:26-28.

In the previous section, we argued that it is a biblical imperative and privilege for each generation to commission the next generation to go forth into the world to be fruitful and multiply. God infuses this commission with a blessing that is passed from one generation to the next, and all generations in a household flourish when this blessing is allowed to flow. The struggles evident in the history of intergenerational dynamics in the ANA church might lead us to believe that these biblical principles are "pie in the sky" idealism and not applicable to the real world. However, we envision a path in which this compelling picture of intergenerational blessing and commission can be realized in the ANA church.

Biblical Principles

First, both generations must embrace the truth that together they form one household of faith, as God's blessing is passed on and multiplied from generation to generation. No person, group, or generation appears from thin air. Everyone comes from someone else, and each generation will give rise to another after it. It would be easy to allow language and cultural barriers, substantial as they are, to lead us to devalue or dismiss the intergenerational ties that connect us. However, no generation can fully develop its sense of identity when divorced from its parent generation. Also, our predecessors give us much of the spiritual inheritance that we pass on to our descendants (2 Tim. 1:5). Can we ask the next generation to honor us if we have not honored those before us? Imagine what a rich legacy we would give to our children as they watch us wrestle against many obstacles in order to honor our own parents.

Second, both generations must highly value the blessing that is passed from one generation to the next. In the giving of a blessing, timing is important. Blessings, like inheritances, should not be given prematurely, when the recipients lack the maturity to convert them into a full and fruitful life. It is the prerogative of the parents to decide when their children are ready to receive the blessing.

By way of illustration, I (Dave) learned the value of waiting patiently for the blessing. My church (Harvest Community Church) stayed physically together with our parent church (Alliance Fellowship Church) for fifteen years. For twelve of those years, we were financially and operationally independent from our parent church, yet we stayed together because there was no compelling reason to leave. Despite numerous voices within the congregation urging us to set out on our own, our senior leadership recognized that this context provided a necessary environment for the work that God was developing in us that had nothing to do with our location. Also our partnership in educational ministry would have been negatively affected by a premature departure. Despite many frustrations (on both sides) during those years of remaining together, God honored our decision by causing both generations to grow stronger. When we finally made the decision to relocate to another facility, we left with the full blessing of our parent church. That was a wonderful foundation on which to start writing this next chapter in our story as a church.

Third, just as the Hellenists bore the spiritual fruit of discipleship (Acts 6:3,5) before the leadership multiplied (Acts 6:7), so the second generation must bear spiritual fruit before they seek to gain independence as leaders and as a congregation. Many second-generation leaders focus much on the question of congregational independence. To hijack a line from Shakespeare's *Hamlet*, "To stay or not to stay; that is the question." While it is certainly an important question, it is not the *only* question, nor even the *first* question.

Declaring independence and moving out does not magically confer health and vitality to a congregation. Most of what we hope to do "out there" can and must be learned while we are still "in here." It is tempting to make the previous generation the convenient scapegoat for all of our frustrations. We must discipline ourselves to ask honestly whether the first generation is really to blame for our challenges. The church in Acts 6 had healthy candidates "of good repute, full of the Spirit and of wisdom" (v. 3), ready to take the mantle of leadership when opportunity demanded, because they had spent time cultivating healthy leaders within the ministry before seeking out independence.

Finally, the question of whether to stay or remain together should be answered according to the call of God and God's purposes for his kingdom. The formation of a thriving household—whether as an individual family or as a church—is a costly and time-consuming pursuit, but one very much worth pursuing. The process of building a healthy household is one that forms godliness and strength of character in each of the members of that household. It is disingenuous for us to believe that we can bring peace to the world around us if we fail to establish peace within our own households. Second-generation leaders and ministries would do well to commit patiently to building a healthy relationship with the first generation. Such patience, though often exasperating, will shape us into the kind of people who can represent God and thus multiply God's presence and image throughout the world. When both generations have established the household of faith, we will be truly prepared to address the next phase of our relationship.

The question of whether to remain together or not is primarily missional, not logistical or organizational. The two generations form one household over which Christ is the head, and the members of this household must behave and interact in a manner that honors the head of the house. Therefore, whether the two generations remain physically together over time should be a function of calling not personal preference. Each generation's desire and vision must submit to the sovereignty of Christ. In other words, the living arrangement that is finally decided upon must be the one that best furthers Christ's purposes for each generation. In some cases, this will mean remaining together, and in others it will mean a parting of ways.

Multiple Models

Myopic focus on a certain organizational model of first- and second-generation ministry can cause us to forget our call to honor one another in the process of building up the church. However, as we establish a healthy household with open communication, the two generations can take an honest and constructive approach to exploring the nature of their future relationship. In some cases, they will serve God's purposes best by staying together, in others by launching out in different directions. The point is not to hold up either of these arrangements as a prescriptive model; instead, each is a descriptive story that springs out of the specific context and calling of that particular household of faith.

On the surface, Open Door Presbyterian Church (ODPC) in northern Virginia and Harvest Community Church (HCC) in Chicago's northwest suburbs may seem to represent two very different models. The two generations at ODPC have committed to remain physically together, while HCC recently relocated away from its parent church into a different rented facility.[10] However, despite the apparent differences between the two churches, they share one key characteristic in common. Both churches worked very hard and over many years to establish a strong and healthy relationship between the two generations. As with all ANA churches, ODPC and HCC faced their fair share of obstacles, but they leaned into these barriers and worked through them. In both cases, the process of building a multigenerational household of faith was one measured in years, not months.

Our heart's prayer is that ANA Christians and leaders would move forward with the unqualified blessing of their immigrant church background, regardless of the model of church that might be pursued. Also our prayer is that ANA Christians would honor and respect their roots, refusing to expose unnecessarily the failings of their past but courageously drawing from the strengths of the immigrant generation's prayer, sacrifice, and service. The present challenge of intergenerational ministry is an "Acts 6" moment for us; only as we deal with the context of our present challenges will we see God's blessing released most fully.

Practical Steps

Although we have tried to weave practical application throughout our biblical-theological discussion, a few concluding points of application are in order here. First, both generations must remain committed to regular communication. Conflict and misunderstanding may lead second-generation leaders to retreat and avoid further dialogue with the first generation. While such a move may provide temporary relief, it is not a long-term solution. Assumptions and errors thrive when communication wanes. It is helpful to remember that both generations ultimately have the same desire to glorify Christ by building his body.

Second, next-generation ANA leaders would do well to focus on church *health* rather than church *independence*. Whether we gain autonomous control over our own congregations is secondary to whether those congregations are healthy and functional expressions of the body of Christ. The struggles of many post-colonial nations in the African subcontinent teach us that the granting of independence does not magically confer the ability to thrive. Second-generation congregations that seek premature independence struggle unnecessarily. The crisis moment in Acts 6 was overcome not only because the Hebraic leadership delegated leadership to the Hellenists but also because the Hellenistic Christians had been developing mature disciples before this crisis struck the church.

If we believe that a church is people, not programs, policies, and processes, then we must assess church health accordingly. An ANA congregation may have all of its strategic, programmatic, and administrative ducks in a row, but the true measure of its health is its people. Do our second-generation congregations only look good on paper, or are our people thriving and living out their callings, individually and corporately? Before we are *called* the church, we must learn to *be* the church. Too often next generation leaders play the blame game, pointing to the first generation's restrictive policies or lack of empowerment as the reason why they are less than healthy. While it may be true that, in some extreme cases, the first generation is genuinely having a deleterious effect on the second, the latter leaders must not be too quick to pull the blame card. Effective leadership must make the most of adversity and maximize limited resources. ANA leaders and congregations must work hard to make the most of their present situations before seeking independence as a magic bullet.

Thus far we have spoken of church health in very general and abstract terms. It would be helpful to identify and develop tools that would help ANA Christians and leaders more objectively measure the health of their congregations, and it is important that such assessment tools be sensitive to the peculiarities of the ANA context. We also strongly recommend that younger ANA leaders actively seek out peer mentors who have walked a few steps ahead of them and can serve as guides.

Finally, ANA leaders should study the stories of exemplary ANA churches, not merely mimic them as models. There is certainly no shortage of church models for young ANA leaders to draw from. Specific churches should not be held up as templates for success, since their achievements did not come from a formulaic recipe but through practices and convictions forged in the context of ministry. Their victories and successes are often the high points of a journey that included many failures and mistakes as well. No other group trying to reproduce their results can ever retrace the exact path. Young ANA pastors and congregations may be better off exploring what values and principles informed the choices that led to their success. Furthermore, we can learn to draw from stories whose context most closely resembles our own.[11] Models can be derailed when unexpected variables are introduced that knock them off course.

Biblical principles, however, can transcend specific circumstances and guide a young pastor or congregation to keep moving forward even when they find themselves in unfamiliar waters. Throughout this chapter, we have articulated principles inherent within the matrix of blessing, multiplication, and kingdom to guide leaders as they move forward.

In their book *Made to Stick*, authors Chip Heath and Dan Heath describe a military principle known as Commander's Intent (CI).[12] CI is a clear, concise, and simple statement of the overall objective a commander has for a particular mission or operation. It equips the soldiers on the ground to adjust fluidly to changing conditions on the battlefield without losing sight of the objective. This idea can be helpful when considering how one church can benefit from the example of another. If Jesus is our commanding officer (2 Tim. 2:4), what are his highest-level intentions for the church? What principles and convictions will guide us in the right direction even when our situations change or we meet with unexpected obstacles and unforeseen opposition?

Viewing exemplary churches through the lens of stories rather than role models or template also allows ANA leaders to draw helpful principles and values from more than one source. Rather than being bound by a single model that may need to be abandoned when it no longer fits reality, these leaders can collect the best principles and values from a wide range of examples and apply them to their own situations.

Conclusion

Returning to our opening illustration, how could Pastor Mark seek to honor the first-generation leadership when they changed the direction of the English ministry? "Honor your father and mother so that it may go well with you in the land that the Lord your God is giving you" (Deut. 5:16). To heed this principle of honoring the parents' generation in the household of God is sometimes difficult. But after praying about the decision, the leaders of the English ministry sought to honor the Korean congregation and focused on cultivating the character qualities and the spiritual growth (fruit) of the core leaders in the English ministry, even if the future of the ministry was unclear.

After a full year of building up the English ministry in this way and seeking to honor the Korean congregation, the Korean governing board invited the leadership of the English ministry to a meeting and presented a letter in November of 2010. In an apparent reversal of policy, they gave their full blessing for the English ministry to become a fully functioning church. The following is an excerpt from the letter from the Korean governing board:

> Although our English congregation exists as a ministry in the Korean Church, the congregation grows far larger [sic] to be simply a ministry within a church. We believe, everybody agrees, the pastoral leadership has reached its full maturity to carry on the command from Jesus Christ by themselves. Also, we found the membership is full of many faithful, the pure-minded and the dedicated. It has been actually our joy to watch the vibrant group blossoming in Jesus. Hallelujah! Also we estimate that the English congregation is very close to self-sufficiency in finance. If this was a church planting, it would be a very successful one. There could be a standalone, fully independent church serving Jesus by now. The Korean Church leadership feels like proud parents watching a mature child fully grown ready to take on the world. . . . The previous policy of the governing board has been one governing body with two ministries and that the English and Korean congregations grow together to a larger scale. However, through the contacts between the leaderships and members of two congregations, this new approach has emerged.

The English congregation received this blessing to become an independent church with deep gratitude, and a new church was formally birthed on April 24, 2011. In sum, this letter released God's blessing from the parent's generation for the multiplication of the next generation so that the work of God's kingdom might be extended in our area. Although the process of honoring this biblical matrix of blessing, multiplication, and kingdom was both laborious and painful, it has been instrumental in preparing and training our church for its distinct contribution to its area.

The realities of ministry in any context are messy, and answers are rarely simple. While considering multiple models for ministry is viable, we must ultimately hold to biblical principles. When we honor our parents' generation and draw from their legacy of faith and sacrifice, then God's blessing is more fully released to us so that we might bring hope through the church to our broken world. Though the process of seeing God's blessing passed from generation to generation is often both painful and frustrating, we circumvent the difficulties and complexities of living as God's household at our own peril. May God's blessing from the parents' generation be fully released to the next generation for the greatest expansion of God's kingdom.

✦
NOTES

1. This survey of texts is brief and limited in scope. While other texts relate more generally to this theme (e.g., Eph. 5:21–6:4; 1 Tim. 5:1-2), our goal is not to develop a comprehensive biblical theology of intergenerational ministry but rather to trace out one trajectory in the story of the Bible and explore how it is fulfilled. This trajectory will begin in Genesis 1:28 and trace how this language, specifically "be fruitful and multiply," is used throughout the Bible.

2. Similarly, the historical-cultural background of the ancient Near East corroborates this understanding, as images served as representatives of God or the king on earth. The *tselem* functions in the absence of the king to demonstrate the king's rule in a certain area. See further in J. Richard Middleton, *The Liberating Image: The Imago Dei in Genesis 1* (Grand Rapids: Brazos, 2005), 93–145.

3. In Genesis 3, a serpent enters the garden. Instead of subduing the serpent, Adam and Eve are subdued by the serpent's duplicity and eat of the fruit from the forbidden tree. The serpent is later interpreted as Satan (Rev. 12:9). Dominion was to be exercised not only over the animals but also over evil forces in the world (cf. Gen. 4:6-7).

4. Notice that the combination "fill" and "earth" occur in both Habakkuk 2:14 and Genesis 1:28.

5. Bill Hybels calls such a leader a "360 degree" leader—leading not only those under us but also those who are at our same level and those above us.

See Bill Hybels, *Courageous Leadership* (Grand Rapids: Zondervan, 2002), 181–98.

6. The connection with Genesis 1:28 is heightened when we observe that Acts 7:17 quotes a reiteration of Genesis 1:28 in Exodus 1:7, "The people increased and multiplied in Egypt" (ESV). The connections between these texts can be seen in greater detail in I. Howard Marshall, "Acts" in *Commentary on the New Testament Use of the Old* (Grand Rapids: Baker Academic, 2007).

7. The importance of the natural family can be seen in that the jailer's whole household is saved (Acts 16:31), the faith of Lois is passed down from generation to generation (2 Tim. 1:4-5), the church is described as the household of God (Eph. 6), and relationships within the church are described in familial terms (1 Tim. 5:1).

8. The apocryphal work *Joseph and Aseneth* reflects the attempt to justify this assimilation by drawing upon the marriage of Joseph to an Egyptian.

9. Andrew Walls's article "The Ephesian Moment" is instructive in how we understand the reconciliation of multiple cultural expressions that constitute the Ephesian church. See Andrew Walls, "The Ephesian Moment," in *The Cross-Cultural Process in Christian History* (Maryknoll, NY: Orbis, 2002).

10. At the ANA consultation at Trinity Evangelical Divinity School in May 2009, the external differences between ODPC and HCC became an interesting source of conversation, as Asian American pastors and leaders discussed intergenerational ministry with differing church models. The ongoing discussion revealed the importance of focusing on biblical principles undergirding the process of ministry instead of the external product and model of ministry. The story of ODPC can be found in Peter Cha, Paul Kim, and Dihan Lee, "Multigenerational Households," in *Growing Healthy Asian American Churches* (Downers Grove: InterVarsity, 2006), 164–82.

11. Stories of such churches can be found in many places. The story of ODPC is referred to in note 10. Another story can be found in Peter Cha, "Constructing New Intergenerational Ties, Cultures and Identities among Korean-American Christians: A Congregational Case Study," in *This Side of Heaven: Race, Ethnicity and Christian Faith*, ed. Robert J. Priest and Alvaro L. Nieves (Oxford: Oxford University Press, 2007), 259–74.

12. The US Army realized that battle plans often became useless ten minutes into the battle. This is because the enemy does not follow the plan but acts on its own. When the opposing force threw off the "script," troops and officers on the ground became paralyzed about what to do next. The commander's intent distills the entire battle plan into a simple statement that gives soldiers the freedom and flexibility to improvise without getting off track. See Chip Heath and Dan Heath, *Made to Stick* (New York: Random House, 2007), 24–28.

✝

CHAPTER 3

The Disillusioned Generation

Ecclesiology from the Margins

GIDEON TSANG AND
SOONG-CHAN RAH

Pastor John sits at his desk reflecting on the previous night's leadership meeting. Not only last night, but for the past few meetings, John has left with a deep sense of frustration. It seemed that most of his young leaders were disillusioned, cynical, and hypercritical about the church. They were involved in the church but seemingly disinterested in making long-term commitments and unable to stay focused on the everyday aspects of church life. John was becoming increasingly impatient with the angst that seemed to be a salient characteristic of the twentysomething generation. His frustration grew as these young leaders raised issues and questions that seemed to divert from the real important issues and the foundational work of the church. At the same time, Pastor John recognized that many of their peers had already left the church, voting with their feet against the organized church. Their disillusionment had led to their disenfranchisement.

The week before in the Sunday sermon, Pastor John had raved to his congregation about his admiration for the latest NBA rookie sensation who had brought an edge to the game and jolted the rest of the team out of its complacency. John had proceeded to preach that it was this type of out-of-the box thinking that was needed in an institution like the church. Pablo Picasso, Frank Lloyd Wright, Albert Einstein, and Amelia Earhart, claimed Pastor John, were individuals who challenged convention and brought about much-needed change. Great innovative thinkers, John claimed, led by challenging the status quo and applying innovation and a new way of thinking. Unfortunately, navigating relationships with such innovative and challenging thinkers was proving to be more difficult than Pastor John had anticipated.

While the image of the church as a household or a family system evokes a sense of functional, healthy unity, the actual experience of church often feels quite dysfunctional and unhealthy. To those who desire the church to be a full, healthy expression of the household of God, this contradiction raises the question, "What relationships within God's household lead to dysfunction?" Peter Steinke, in *Congregational Leadership in Anxious Times*, examines family systems and seeks to understand "what happens when people come together and interact, how they mutually influence each other's behaviors, how change in one person affects another, and how they create something larger than themselves."[1] In other words, family systems have the capacity to take on a life of their own and influence and transform those within that system. Furthermore, Edwin Friedman asserts that family systems can influence other systems within the church. Friedman speaks of three interlocking systems: "The families within the congregation, our congregations, and our own [families]. Because the emotional process in all of these systems is identical, unresolved issues in any of them can produce symptoms in the others."[2]

Both Steinke and Friedman see the critical role of family systems and the interconnected nature of relationships. As we explore the theme of the household and family of God, we need to see that dysfunction in the system is not a result of only one aspect of the system (e.g., those we label as the disillusioned), but instead reflects the reality of the potential dysfunction of all aspects of the system. In fact, the outliers and the marginalized in the system (e.g., young leaders restless for change) are often the best indicators of the problems within the household. Any discussion about the disillusioned generation has to take into account the systemic dysfunction within the household and the potentially positive role that the disillusioned may ultimately play in the family system.

The biblical metaphor of family can be at best beautifully inclusive but at worst painfully exclusive. In the biblical story of the prodigal son (Luke 15:11-32), we encounter a dysfunctional family system. The family experiences trauma and conflict as the younger son introduces anxiety into the family system. The rebellious actions of the prodigal son mean that the harmony and *shalom* of the household has been shattered. It is the exemplary and gracious behavior of the father that restores the family. For many Asian North American (ANA) congregations, the story of the prodigal son has been used to describe the wayward nature of the disillusioned second generation. In exploring the disillusioned generation, a common misinterpretation depicts the first-generation immigrant churches as the father in the parable—patiently waiting for the return of the lost generation. Accurate exegesis, however, requires that the father in the story represents God, our gracious heavenly Father.

A key element of the parable that is often neglected is the role of the older brother. The older brother provides the contrast to the younger brother, and both brothers provide valuable insight into the grace of God. Thus, if the second generation is projected as the prodigal son in the story, the first generation should be projected as the older brother. When applying the parable to the ANA church, it becomes a story about the dysfunctional family system of the ANA church—not merely as a challenge to the disillusionment of the second generation (the younger brother), but also to the judgment and rigidity of the first generation (the older brother).

Our biblical and theological reflection of the disillusioned generation requires prophetic imagination moving us beyond simple categories. It is easy to mark a generation with a pejorative label, but it is part of the responsibility of the previous generation to seek to understand the prophetic challenge that the disillusioned generation may bring. The disillusioned are those who feel excluded, not because of primary theological differences but simply because of cultural (both ethnic and generational) barriers. To be a healthy household of God, the intentional inclusion of the "disillusioned" is vital; they are part of the family of faith. Indeed, we believe that "the excluded disillusioned" have great gifts and potentially prophetic perspectives to offer to the ANA church.

Who and What Are the "Disillusioned"?

When the Catalyst Consultation on ANA Theology and Ministry convened, those who were assigned the topic of the disillusioned generation were confronted with the immediate problem of defining their task and the phrase "disillusioned generation." Consistent with what the term provokes, negative responses and definitions immediately emerged from the group:

"They have everything going for them. . . . Why are they not happy with their lives?"

"They seem to be just wandering in life."

"They've seen a lot but just don't seem to be motivated."

"They're at the church but aren't really involved."

"They are consumers more than participants."

These types of initial gut reactions were common. The group was already making the mistake of casting quick judgment without first attempting to understand what it actually means to be disillusioned. The immediate negative connotation created a sense of "us versus them" and pushed the trajectory of the conversation toward a negative, polarized, almost confrontational model. Our first task became the work of unpacking what we mean by the "disillusioned generation."

For the purposes of this chapter, we have drawn upon input from that group to form a single definition. The disillusioned generation is comprised essentially of the de-churched[3] among the next generation of the ANA population,[4] who are predominantly in their twenties and thirties.[5] The disillusioned generation reveals both generational issues as well as issues within the age group. Working from this definition, we can begin to formulate ways in which the ANA church can respond to its de-churched. Out of the specific context of the ANA church, we can discern an application for the household of God found in various contexts throughout North America.

The concept of disillusionment with the church appears to be part of a larger phenomenon in North American evangelicalism. For example, in 2009 the *Christian Science Monitor* published a series of articles by the late blogger Michael Spencer, the so-called Internet monk (www.theinternetmonk.com). In "The Coming Evangelical Collapse," Spencer observes, "We Evangelicals have failed to pass on to our young people an orthodox form of faith that can take root and survive the secular onslaught."[6] The Spencer article (among others appearing at about the same time) pointed to the ways that North American Christianity, particularly evangelicalism, is threatened by a diminishing involvement of the younger generation.

Two different studies in 2008—the American Religious Identification Survey (ARIS) and a study by the Pew Forum on Religion and Public Life[7]—attest to the growing cynicism toward American Christianity. According to the ARIS study, "The U.S. population continues to show signs of becoming less religious, with one out of every five Americans failing to indicate a religious identity in 2008."[8] The fastest-growing category for Americans is the rapidly increasing number of those who view themselves as "spiritual but not religious." As a popular book title among evangelicals asserts, *They Love Jesus but Not the Church*.[9]

With the growth edge of American Christianity coming from immigrant, ethnic minority, and multiethnic churches, the way the gospel is translated into these communities provides important information on the ongoing work of reaching succeeding generations. In other words, the next evangelicalism requires lessons from one another in the broader Christian community.[10] Responding to this decline requires unity in the body of Christ, even as we consider specificity and particularity in how the gospel message is reaching different people groups and generations.

Specifically from the ANA Christian community, emerging stories of disillusionment begin to inform the sense of disillusionment on a larger scale. In our gathering of ANA leaders, pastors, and parachurch workers, a number of stories and themes emerged to describe (from the outside and from the inside) the disillusioned generation. The following phrases indicate the reflections and insights offered by this generation:

"We haven't found connection or felt welcome at the traditional church."

"We have experienced too much church in-fighting and hypocrisy."

"Our disillusionment leads to depression—that things are never going to change."

"We see the dysfunction of an immigrant church teaching an American dream that doesn't fit with biblical values."

"We are realists asking questions."

"We are trying to create new wineskins."

While these comments emerge out of the ANA Christian context, they certainly have an application and overlap with issues arising out of the larger context of North American Christianity.

As we reflect on these sobering reports (both anecdotal and statistical) in light of the theology of the household of God and the parable of the prodigal son, interesting insights emerge. In the household of God, a family system is at work. The family system reveals two different expressions of human sinfulness. The younger brother displays a rebellious spirit that results in his departure and his separation from the loving father. The older brother displays a prideful spirit that results in a separation from the gracious father and from the prodigal brother. Our tendency may be to focus on the sinful actions of the younger brother. While the younger brother's actions are not to be excused, the sinful actions of the older brother must also be taken seriously.

We should also consider that the prodigal serves the role of revealing the fallen nature of the older brother. We can discern that the disillusioned generation operates as prodigals, but what if the prodigals have an important story to tell and a lesson to teach the household of God? What if "we" who are the older brothers in the story—those who have remained in the household and have served faithfully at home—are willing to hear the lesson in the parable directed toward the older brother, rather than jumping to the need to teach the younger brother a lesson? This lesson of grace arises from a depth of theological reflection on the household of God, leading to an ethic of unity that leads to the revival of the Christian community.

Theological Framework for the Dysfunctional System

As stated in chapter 1, grace provides the foundation, core nature, and healthy functioning of the household of God. Without grace, the household of God does not exist, since we are adopted into God's family through grace. Since the household began with the foundation of grace, should not the ongoing development of the family of God also be characterized by grace? What then, does grace look like in the context of a household of God that is dealing with a prodigal child? In contrast to the older brother who displayed a lack of grace, can all parties (both the older brother and the younger brother) be the recipients of the grace we desperately need? In relation to the father, all parties are in need of grace: the first-generation immigrant whose ministries have flourished, the second-generation ANAs who have remained in the church, and the de-churched, disillusioned next-generation ANAs who left the church in significant numbers.

Furthermore, the core nature of the household of God is unity, on which the survival of a family depends. "If a house is divided against itself, that house will not be able to stand" (Mark 3:25, NRSV; also Matt. 12:25; Luke 11:17). To live into the fullness of being God's household requires an authentic unity of all members of the household. The biblical call for the church to be the household of God necessitates the need for reconciliation in the church across the generations and tearing down the dividing wall of hostility between church and unchurched, between first and second generation, and between insider and outsider (see Eph. 2:11-21). Being the household of God moves us to a radical grace that calls for the inclusion of the disillusioned generation.

Biblical Metaphors to Guide Us

Brothers (and sisters). Working from the younger brother and older brother motif in the parable, we see an Old Testament example of the younger brother bringing correction and restoration to the older brother(s). The story of Joseph in the book of Genesis reveals the role of a younger brother in bringing healing and hope for his entire household (Gen. 37ff.). The arrogance of Joseph leads to his rejection by his older brothers (Gen. 37). Despite this rejection (and maybe because of it), Joseph is taken from his home and sent to a distant place, ultimately to find success in the secular world (Gen. 41). After finding success in that other world, the younger brother is able to bring a blessing to his entire household (Gen. 45–47). Members of the disillusioned generation, therefore, are not to be rejected as having no contribution to make to the household of God, but instead seen as important contributors—and maybe even a part of the redemption of the entire household.

Resident aliens. Another biblical-theological motif that aids our approach to the disillusioned generation is the concept of the resident alien. The New Testament alludes to Christians having citizenship in heaven and not on earth (Phil. 3:20). Our household therefore is ultimately a heavenly one, not an earthly household. "Our citizenship is transferred from one dominion to another, and we become, in whatever culture we find ourselves, resident aliens."[11] The potential contribution of the disillusioned generation is to remind the established church of that calling to be a resident alien. Disillusionment may take many different forms, but if it arises out of a recognition that the institutional church has become captive to the norms of the dominant culture, then the disillusioned generation can serve the church by revealing sinful patterns.

An ongoing battle in the North American evangelical church is the struggle to understand the relationship between the church and the culture. While the gospel message needs to be contextualized in order to be relevant to the culture, the church in the West has often become captive to the culture, rather than finding ways to be prophetic to the culture. The North American church has a history of failing to relate positively to its cultural surroundings. The North American church has vacillated between antagonism toward the culture or becoming too enmeshed with culture. Immigrant churches have the dual temptation of becoming too enmeshed with their home cultural values, while at the same time becoming enamored by their host country's value system. The ANA church needs to recover the sense of being an alien colony in the world.

Wineskins. Already strangers in a new world, immigrants may cling to the values of their homeland rather than adhering to the values of faith in Jesus Christ. Captivity to the values of majority culture and nostalgia for homeland culture can quickly become the old wineskin that prevents a new generation from experiencing the fullness of God's work in the world. In Luke 5:33-39, Jesus reveals that new wine cannot be poured into old wineskins; new wineskins are needed for new wine. A generation that may be disillusioned by old wineskins in the church can provide the necessary example of the "resident alien," which exposes the inadequacy of the old wineskin.[12] The disillusioned generation, therefore, has the potential to issue a challenge to the church to employ new wineskins.

Prophetic voices. The potential positioning of the disillusioned generation as resident aliens and as new wineskins offers the hope of a prophetic role for this generation. In this chapter, we define "prophetic" as the challenge offered to God's people from within their community. Prophetic challenges offer an alternative perspective from the potential tendency of the church to prioritize maintenance and self-preservation. At the same time, these prophetic challenges should reflect the truth of God's words. True prophecy arises from speaking the words and heart of God, and at times these prophetic enactments may challenge the status quo, calling the community to repent from the sins of the community.

Walter Brueggemann reveals the need for prophetic voices and a prophetic imagination that can properly motivate the disillusioned generation. Brueggemann discusses the difference between the temple worship of the established religious community of Solomon's

Israel versus the tabernacle worship of Mosaic Israel that points toward a new direction.[13] The institutional temple worship of Solomon required static systems and structures (including taxation) to maintain the status quo (1 Kings 5:13-18; 9:15-22). In contrast, under Moses, Israel's worship was a statement of a break from the oppressive powers of Pharaoh (see Exod. 2:23-25; 15:1-18). Israel's worship in the desert was an expression of a prophetic imagination that not only pointed to the dismantling of an oppressive power system but to the future hope of Israel. Prophetic imagination is an important component of God's ongoing redemptive work. "The task of prophetic ministry is to nurture, nourish, and evoke a consciousness and perception alternative to the consciousness and perception of the dominant culture around us."[14] A hope-filled, prophetic imagination becomes a part of the contribution the disillusioned generation offers to the status quo established church.

Hope-Filled Imagination

I (Gideon) hope to build on the sociological and theological foundation that my colleague Soong-Chan has laid above, not so much with more theory, but with lessons learned via my own personal experience. I write as a disillusioned younger "punk brother," whose journey in returning to the father was graciously and patiently nurtured by older siblings such as Paul Tokanaga; Peter Cha; Jeanette Yep; Dan Davis; my first senior pastor, Daniel Shen; and my father. These "older siblings" functioned as persistent counselors and prophetic mentors that transformed my unbridled anger into useful passion.

These leaders had the hope-filled imagination to see disillusionment as leadership potential. They did not spend their time on the theoretical and often condescending conversations on how to fix the disillusioned generation. Instead, these older siblings hoped to see younger siblings like me potentially providing new wineskins of ministry. With such a hope-filled lens, they saw strength when others saw weaknesses. What are some of these perceived weaknesses that can be viewed as potential strengths? I offer the following three discoveries.

Dissatisfaction as a Progressive Recognition of Cracking Old Wineskins

Often what is called disillusionment is actually cynicism toward the immigrant church's unwillingness to deal with real problems. The emperor's new clothes were not clothes but instead an unwillingness of the masses to call out the obvious problem of the king's outfit (or lack thereof). A great deal of reformation needs to take place in the ANA church (as well as the North American church as a whole). In search of new wineskins, too many are trading old existing wineskins—the immigrant church—for different old wineskins, such as large megachurches. Rather than convincing young leaders to fall in line with dysfunction, we need to encourage, give direction to, and nurture their reformation potential that often is expressed as immature grumbling.

I have been a part of immigrant churches that were not only unwilling to serve the poor, but they would chase away the homeless who tried to ask for help. For years I would talk to the church leadership about serving these homeless friends, since God brought them to our front door without avail. In 2006, when we planted our church, one of the first organizations we partnered with was the Austin Resource Center for the Homeless. We invited an activist for the homeless community to speak to our congregation about how the church can better serve these friends in need. In 2008 we opened a community center in an underserved part of the city in our attempts to feed the hungry, clothe the naked, and welcome strangers.

Stubbornness as Potential Confidence in God's Mission and Purpose

Leadership requires a stubborn confidence in what God is doing even if it seems like a miniscule path compared to the wide and well-traveled highways of the masses. Immature stubbornness can be written off because of its inherent arrogance—and at times, that may be an accurate assessment. However, in Scripture we see God taking innovative outliers, such as Moses, Esther, Joseph, Peter, and Paul, through desert experiences that refine them into world-class kingdom leaders.

We have a young man in our community, a young man I will call "Eric." We met him as a young artist angry against institutional Christianity (he still is in some ways). Many of the churches he tried to be a part of in the past rejected his outspoken criticisms of the church. I saw his stubborn criticisms as prophetic potential. In his six years of being a part of our community, God slowly humbled his brash stubbornness through failure, broken relationships, and mistakes made. He is now a missionary in Central Asia in the heart of war and terrorism. We need hope-filled leaders who trust in God's ability to redeem their sinfulness and to imagine the possibility of redemptive leadership that can arise out of an unrefined stubbornness. Ultimately, it reflects a deep trust in God to continue the work of redemption that has begun in them.

Outrageous Ideas as Attempts at Vision and Prophetic Imagination

Ideas can be transformative. In the book *101 Unuseless Japanese Inventions*, Kenji Kawakami describes many innovative examples of Japanese ingenuity, such as mini-umbrellas for your shoes, eyedrop funnels for glasses, and—my personal favorite—the butter glue stick.[15] The genius of Japanese innovation is that among the thousands of bad ideas are a handful of brilliant ones. Visionaries often have more failed ideas than successful ones. We must allow room for these young visionaries to risk failure in order to be successful in God's work in their generation. Our hope is to see the church develop the ability to encourage visionary leadership directed by God. The ANA church should form the disillusioned generation to embody the fullness of prophetic ministry as those with prophetic vision that can direct the church toward God and reflect the will of God for the world.

In the Gospel of Mark (particularly in chapters 8–10), we see numerous failures of the disciples, particularly the apostle Peter. Yet Jesus patiently works to develop disciples who bring earthshaking transformation. In the book of Acts, we begin to see the brash actions of the apostle Peter becoming the actions of a seasoned leader full of courage and conviction. In 1 Peter, we see the expression of mature leadership in Peter's willingness to embrace suffering for the sake of the gospel. We have the responsibility of developing young leaders as the potential-filled generation or losing them as the disillusioned generation.

Strategic Initiatives

Our prayer is that the conversation on disillusionment will turn from a negative deconstructionism toward a hope-filled strategy. So where do we go from here? We offer the following possible strategies.

Champions for the Disillusioned

Leadership reproduction is not a new idea; neither is it biological or hereditary. Rather, it is nurtured and developed. The question we need to ask is, "What kind of leaders are we producing?" In his rookie year for the Milwaukee Bucks, Brandon Jennings unleashed a 55-point outburst against the Golden State Warriors. At least eight NBA teams who passed on him during the draft offered excuses for why passing on Jennings was justifiable (while secretly throwing up on their scouting binders). The big debate among experts was how did so many coaches and general managers not see his potential as a player? Perhaps the only leader who believed in Jennings and his abilities was Sonny Vaccaro, the controversial yet respected high school basketball guru. While everyone saw Jennings as immature, brash, and unreliable, Sonny saw a future franchise point guard.

A great artist has the vision to see a sculpture while others simply see a block of wood. A great musician has the imagination to hear a symphony while others simply hear unrefined noise. And a great leader has the hope to champion those whom others see as disillusioned youngsters.

The name of the church community I have the honor of leading is called Vox Veniae. We are a painfully young and diverse community serving in the lower-income urban landscape of Austin, Texas. In addition to learning how to plant a church, we are trying to run a community art/neighborhood development space (intended to serve a diverse population that includes anarchists, gays, lesbians, bisexuals, transgender persons, and fundamentalist African American Christians) while also running an intentional community of fifteen homes. As hard as it may be to understand our community, perhaps even more shocking is that our church was birthed by an immigrant church. Our core leadership all grew up in Chinese immigrant churches. The story of Vox is the story of God taking a group of left-brained, first-generation engineers and birthing a progressive missional church. The common bystander simply would have seen us as arrogant rebels with dodgy ideas. These glasses-wearing, bowl cut–sporting, Camry-driving, spreadsheet-loving engineers not only envisioned what God could do, but championed our unrefined potential. Through that combination, God graced and orchestrated the birth of Vox Veniae.

Arguably one of the most important gifts a pastor can give is the investment of his or her own life into the lives of the next generation. This commitment to emerging young pastors and leaders does not come without its challenges, at times made more complex for ANAs because of generational differences and expectations and sometimes by the implicit hierarchical relationships. When present, deep commitment to the development of the next generation of leaders is a powerful and empowering sign of the kingdom. It is the gift of believing. It is openness to the new. It is the affirmation of sons and daughters.

Kevin Doi, a third-generation Japanese American and founding pastor of Epic Church in Fullerton, California, was the beneficiary of such investment as a young twentysomething. Cory Ishida, senior pastor of Evergreen Baptist Church of San Gabriel Valley, provided Kevin seed money and the opportunity to plant a different kind of church community, a feat made all the more remarkable given its theological and philosophical departures from Cory's own ministry. Cory's support of this venture without fully understanding the vision or where it would lead shows the rare kind of trust, generosity, and freedom necessary to birth next generation ministries. The other significant source of inspiration and involvement came from Ken Fong, senior pastor of Evergreen Baptist Church of Los Angeles.

Serving as Kevin's primary mentor and teacher, Ken recognized and nurtured Kevin's own calling into vocational ministry, investing in his ethnic, personal, and professional development by providing key opportunities to minister alongside and encouraging rather than discouraging Kevin's unique perspective as a church outsider.

The fact that Ken valued Kevin's background and uncommon path to the ministry as a saving grace rather than something sacrilegious provided the kind of affirmation and acceptance a young leader needs to be oneself and not the image of another. Through Ken's guidance, Kevin was allowed to question, to doubt, to experiment—without the pressure to conform or the expectation to perform in preexisting structures or philosophies of ministry in the ANA church or the wider Western majority Christian context. Because of the personal commitment of Pastors Cory and Ken within more traditional forms of the ANA church, Kevin was given the space to grow, develop his own convictions, and eventually lead a multicultural church in the city pursuing community, justice, and healing. Without the involvement of these two men, this story would not have been possible for Kevin. This is the beauty and fruit of investment—from one generation to the next.

Listening and Communicating

As simple as it sounds, the best mentors are great listeners. My mentors listened to my insane ideas with smiles and nods, not because the ideas were good (most of them were ridiculous) but because they believed in God's grace and God's ability to redeem ridiculous people spouting ridiculous ideas. The weaknesses of my attempts were opportunities for God's greatness. Recall the older brother in the story of the prodigal son. Imagine if *guh-goh* (older brother in Chinese) asked *sai-loh* (younger brother) a simple question: "So, why did you leave?" I believe *guh-goh* would have learned a great deal in hearing *sai-loh's* story. Together they would both better understand the heart of their father.

In July 2007 West Houston Chinese Church (WHCC) sent out a group of its members to start a new church. Far from a church split, the move was a celebration of mission. The leaders of WHCC blessed Ted Law, their English pastor, to become the lead church planter, a move made possible because of a tone of openness and generosity set by senior pastor David Hsu. Ted Law tells his story:

> I remember the moment when Pastor David and I realized we were heading in different directions. We were driving home from a youth camp, and I began sharing with him some of the dreams and ideas I had for ministry. This was nothing new. We shared ideas regularly. Sensing my urgency, though, he asked me when I wanted to start working on new initiatives. I replied with a two- to three-year timeline. He said that he had imagined my ideas for the long haul, fifteen years down the line. That's when we both knew we needed to talk more about the future. WHCC has had a positive track record of healthy leadership and growth. Even so, because its core mission is reaching Chinese, it had a difficult time creating space for second-generation leaders to expand beyond that mission. Pastor David asked me to share my ideas with the elders of the church, asking for their honest feedback.

The discussion wasn't easy at first, but the difficulty was not church planting per se. WHCC was indeed a church plant, and it had a vision to reproduce Chinese churches. But the elders had a hard time accepting Ted's different vision and passion for the church and its reach. This was initially true even for Pastor David. However, during this season, Pastor David attended a church leadership conference where he met a few second-generation ANA pastors. After sitting and listening to their stories, he grew in his understanding and connected with their desires to reach out to those who didn't fit well in a traditional immigrant church. This eventually led to an analogy he shared with the elders of his church: "Suppose you started a new company. Your dream was to create something that you could pass on to your son. However, you woke up one day to realize that he didn't want to manage your company. Instead of inheriting your business, he inherited your love for entrepreneurship. What would you do?"

The story for WHCC concluded with commissioning Ted and a core group to start what has become Access, a church that is reaching out to the disillusioned. This is a story of a humble and secure "older brother church" with a seasoned leader (David Hsu) releasing and blessing the younger brother to start a different kind of church. The path to these beautiful stories of healthy intergenerational relationships must pass through the initial phase of simply listening. Imagine how many more stories we could tell if we could convince more leaders to listen.

Rites of Passage

Throughout history, cultures have different rite of passage ceremonies signifying a celebration into a new phase of life. The ceremony itself has no magical powers but instead marks a moment of significance. In Scripture, baptisms and marriages are examples of ceremonies to help us remember new beginnings. A visionary leader creates such moments as intentional leadership development opportunities. What might leadership ceremonies look like in the twenty-first-century ANA church? Following are two examples:

Ken Kong: God has been doing a great work within the Southeast Asian community. For the past five years, God has brought together leaders from around the nation to form the Southeast Asian Committee (SEAC), and we have successfully hosted two national leadership summits. Our second summit was held in 2008. God continued to bless and encourage us, and even bring healing. During the last night of the summit, a first-generation Cambodian pastor approached me, asking if he could share something that was on his heart. I hesitated and was afraid of what he had to say. So I handed him over to the emcee of the night to investigate. Once the emcee screened him, the Cambodian pastor was allowed to share. And am I glad he did.

The Cambodian pastor shared about how God had knocked him in the head and revealed to him a simple message: that the first-generation leaders needed to release the next generation into ministry, to repent and ask for forgiveness for their ways of holding back the next generation from being led by the Lord. As he repented and asked for forgiveness on behalf of the first generation, God came down and touched our hearts. He ministered and brought healing to the next generation, blessing and empowering us to move forward in him and with him.

Sharon Koh: My senior pastor believes that people with power need to give it away. I've heard him say this on many occasions, but it was most clearly said to me on the day I was ordained. In many of our mentoring conversations, Ken would talk about his days at Fuller Theological Seminary. Many of the brightest and most talented students he would meet were women, Asian women. Yet, despite their consistent excellence in the classroom, many of these women did not receive the same career opportunities as their male counterparts.

Ken is one of these people who first saw tremendous potential in a young female seminarian and then held some doors open. At my ordination, in front of a few hundred guests and representatives from our denomination, Ken told me: "I believe someday you will be senior pastor of a church. On that day and on the days from now until then, make sure you give the grace given to you away."

I know that my experience is different from that of many others. Ken is the second senior pastor I've worked with who affirmed my call to pastoral ministry. I can only imagine that the grace I've been given makes it my responsibility to give more of such grace away. I am convinced that it gives God great pleasure to see his children treating each other this way.[16]

Two years into planting Vox Veniae, one of my mentors made an astute observation. He said to me, "Gideon, it is clear that you know who you *do not* want to be as a church: the question is, however, who is God calling you to be? You have spent enough time deconstructing; now construct something. Don't just tear down. Create!"

That's good advice. As important as deconstruction is, it needs to lead to construction. We have spent enough time deconstructing what this "disillusioned generation" is and who we do not want its members to be. Now the better question is, who is God calling them to be, and how can we participate in that process?

Our hope is that this generation's disillusioned deconstruction of conventional church will ultimately give way to God's construction of healthy households, developing creative, innovative leaders for the future.

✦
NOTES

1. Peter L. Steinke, *Congregational Leadership in Anxious Times* (Herndon, VA: Alban Institute, 2006), xi.

2. See Edwin H. Friedman, *Generation to Generation* (New York: Guilford, 1985).

3. The de-churched are individuals who have previously attended church or have been affiliated with a church but have left the church, most likely altogether. They are likely to have no current church involvement at all.

4. For the purpose of our discussion, we focus on the Asian North American (ANA) population. Specifically, we focus on the English-speaking, second, and next generation of the ANA church.

5. While being "disillusioned" is not limited to one specific age group, the generational aspect of ANA ministry means that the majority of this group would be individuals in their twenties and thirties.

6. Michael Spencer, "The Coming Evangelical Collapse," *The Christian Science Monitor* (March 10, 2009), under "Why Is This Going to Happen?," www.csmonitor.com/Commentary/Opinion/2009/0310/p09s01-coop.html (accessed March 14, 2011).

7. One glaring flaw in these studies and in books based on them is that they focus on trends reflecting the declining number and decreasing role of white evangelical Christians in America. However, the changing demographics of North American society in general and of North American Christianity in particular require that we broaden our perspective on understanding the dynamics of reaching multiple generations with the gospel.

8. Barry A. Kosmin and Ariela Keysar, *American Religious Identification Survey* (Hartford, CT: Trinity College Press, 2009), 2.

9. Dan Kimball, *They Love Jesus but Not the Church* (Grand Rapids: Zondervan, 2007).

10. See Soong-Chan Rah, *The Next Evangelicalism: Freeing the Church from Western Cultural Captivity* (Downers Grove, IL: InterVarsity, 2009).

11. Stanley Hauerwas and William H. Willimon, *Resident Alien: Life in the Christian Colony* (Nashville: Abingdon, 1989), 12.

12. Sangeeta R. Gupta, *A Quick Guide to Cultural Competency* (India: Gupta Consulting Group, 2007), 20. Cultures that tend to rely on indirect communication (including Asian culture) tend to prioritize the maintenance of "harmony, or at least the appearance of harmony." Because of this tendency, Asian North American culture gravitates toward conflict avoidance and minimizes differences and dissension, yielding a cultural resistance toward any group that displays outlier or anomalous perspectives.

13. Walter Brueggemann, *The Prophetic Imagination*, 2nd ed. (Minneapolis: Fortress, 2001), 1ff.; see especially "The Alternative Community of Moses" (1–20) and "The Royal Consciousness" (21–38).

14. Brueggemann, *Prophetic Imagination*, 3.

15. Kenji Kawakami, *101 Unuseless Japanese Inventions*, ed. Hugh Fearnley-Whittingstall, trans. Dan Papia (New York: W. W. Norton, 2000).

16. Rev. Sharon T. Koh is senior associate pastor of Mission and Community Life at Evergreen Baptist Church of Los Angeles.

CHAPTER 4

✝

Now-Generation Ministry

SAM S. KIM AND
M. SYDNEY PARK

It was supposed to be a quiet Monday morning of rest and recuperation after a full weekend of ministry, but the breaking headline news left me shocked and scrambling for my cell phone. In the spring of 2007, the entire nation was gripped by the shooting massacre at Virginia Tech University. The gunman killed thirty-two people and wounded many more (during two separate attacks about two hours apart on April 16, 2007) before committing suicide, making it the deadliest school shooting in US history.[1] Immediately, I (Sam) began calling each of my former youth group students enrolled at Virginia Tech to confirm their safety and well-being. Thankfully, all of my former students were absent from the buildings where the shootings occurred.

I couldn't help but wonder: "Who would commit such an unthinkable act?" When the gunman's identity as a Korean American was finally disclosed (twenty-three-year-old Seung-Hui Cho), I was burdened and heartbroken. It came to light that several of my students had personally known the gunman both in high school and college. And we even had a family in our church who was related, albeit distantly, to the gunman. Furthermore, I realized that I had attended the young man's high school graduation ceremony since he attended the same local high school as some of my former students.

I had to ask myself: "Did I unwittingly cross paths with Seung-Hui? If so, did I have or make an opportunity to get to know him and care for him with Christ's love?" My heart continued to break when the *Washington Post* reported that this young Korean American man and his family had reached out to local Korean American churches in our area seeking help for their son's emotional and mental instability. And a local Korean American church pastor had indeed ministered to the student and his family, but to no avail.[2]

This one Asian American family's struggle to find critical help for their child from the local Asian North American (ANA) church during his high school years underscores the concerns we hope to address in this chapter. Is the local ANA church able to meet the complex spiritual, emotional, and mental challenges of raising and nurturing healthy children in the twenty-first century? Or is the ANA church frequently playing the role of a glorified baby-sitter while ill-equipped and unprepared to face the weightier issues? What can awaken local church to the desperate needs of children and youth (ages four to eighteen) and to equip their ministry leaders to address those needs effectively?[3]

These concerns cannot be considered secondary. The time to re-think and restructure student ministry is not tomorrow, but today. Often children (including teens) are mislabeled as the "next" generation. This misunderstanding perpetuates the wrong impression: that human beings do not require the full attention of the church until they are adults. However, the church must champion the cause and unleash the resources to help transform the hearts, minds, and souls of our children and youth *now*. Unless the church envisions and approaches children's and youth ministry as the "now generation," we will always be one step behind in fulfilling the explicit mandate Jesus gave to his disciples: "Go therefore and make disciples of all nations, baptizing them in the name of the Father and of the Son and of the Holy Spirit, teaching them to observe all that I have commanded you" (Matt. 28:18-20, ESV).

In the Great Commission, Jesus does not suggest that the church should disciple *only* foreign nations, but *all* nations, including our own (see chapter 9 of this volume). You identify your own nation by considering the people closest to you—those entrusted most nearly to your nurture and discipleship. Thus, for youth ministers, the fulfillment of Christ's commission begins with children and youth. And discipleship begins with the gospel message of God's saving grace in Jesus Christ. Then the question that needs to be addressed is: how does "salvation by grace" shape children's and youth ministry? As it will be evident below, this seemingly simple question rebuffs a unilateral solution. A grace-centered theology and praxis require a multidimensional approach that integrates various relationships in our ministry with the now generation.

Key Issues and Challenges in ANA Children's and Youth Ministry

It has become widely accepted by most children's and youth ministry leaders that effective spiritual discipleship and transformative Christian education is holistic.[4] A holistic youth ministry does not focus only on the needs of the young people, but must necessarily foster healthy partnership with the entire family unit and all levels of church leadership. These three levels of relationship must be maintained simultaneously if we are to minister effectively to the students.[5]

In the sixteen years I (Sam) have served in children's and youth ministry, I have had the privilege of serving in diverse ministry contexts in different geographical settings, occupying various leadership positions. Throughout my varied experiences, I see how significant now-generation ministry issues are, as they span ethnic, cultural, socioeconomic, and geographic boundaries. To help build these bridges, we must begin by understanding and underscoring universal issues and challenges faced by children's and youth ministry in the twenty-first century. Then we can move forward in harnessing the strengths and learning from the weaknesses of children's and youth ministry in ANA ministry contexts.

The greatest universal challenge facing the now generation is the genuine transfer of personal faith and spiritual maturity that extends beyond their adolescent years.[6] Unfortunately, the majority of research and recent surveys often paint a discouraging spiritual landscape and grim outlook. Kara Powell, executive director of the Fuller Youth Institute, highlights the results of Rainer Research that estimate that 70 percent of young people leave the church by the age of twenty-two. The Barna Group Research asserts that this figure increases to 80 percent by the age of thirty. Similarly, Fuller Youth Institute's research discovered that 40 to 50 percent of youth group seniors struggle to continue their faith and connect with their local faith community beyond their high school years.[7] Even without these statistics, one only has to look in the vacant pews of students' home churches to validate the data.

As a whole, the ANA church must remember that ministry to our children is one of the key mandates in the covenant relationship with God: "Hear, O Israel: The LORD our God, the LORD is one. You shall love the LORD your God with all your heart and with all your soul and with all your might. And these words that I command you today shall be on your heart. You shall teach them diligently to your children, and shall talk of them when you sit in your house, and when you walk by the way, and when you lie down, and when you rise" (Deut. 6:4-7, ESV). This passage indicates that children's and youth ministry is central to the health of the covenant community. A faithful application of this passage requires not only reassessment of children's and youth ministry, but reevaluation of the importance of leadership to the young. This change in perspective must occur on three fronts: (1) church leadership (pastoral and lay), (2) children's and youth ministers, and (3) parents. As the now-generation leaders sense that their ministry is an irreplaceable and invaluable component among other ministries within the church, they will be strengthened and encouraged to persevere and serve with joy.

Where to Begin?

How can the church create a healthier atmosphere and culture for a more effective faith transfer to our children and youth? The keys are *partnership* and *mentorship*—stronger partnership within local church leadership (both lay and pastoral) and hands-on parental mentorship at home.

Partnership

Even with a growing demand for children's and youth ministers in churches across the country, the attrition rate among them continues to rise. Many start their ministry careers with tremendous passion and zeal but often give up and move on before they can see the fruit of their labor. When leadership turns over every six months to three years, it is extremely difficult—nearly impossible—for youth workers to cultivate healthy relationships, innovative ministry, and spiritual influence among their students.

The reasons for this quick turnover may of course vary with each case, but two most common factors can be identified. First, most children's and youth leaders struggle with isolation and discouragement from lack of tangible support (spiritual, moral, financial, facility space and scheduling, etc.) from their ministry peers and their senior church leadership. Second, children's and youth ministry is often perceived as a "stepping stone" ministry, delegated to those who need to gain ministry experience before advancing to "real" ministry to adults.[8] This is especially true in the ANA church context, where children and teens are often viewed as "second-class citizens" and their ministers are perceived as part-time workers and apprentices.[9]

These two factors work together to create instability in children's and youth ministry. If the leadership for the "now" generation is a revolving door, the natural consequence is failure to instill genuine and lasting faith in children and youth.[10] Hope for reversing this trend lies in strong partnerships within church leadership. How?

1. For youth leaders who feel ill-equipped and isolated, partnership offers stronger relationships and greater integration in the larger church mission, as well as increased awareness and communication around sharing resources (human and financial).

2. For youth leaders who see their role as a stepping stone to "real" ministry, partnerships offer opportunities for true apprenticeship for those who will ultimately answer a call to senior church leadership, as well as opportunities to affirm their *real* ministry *now*.

Mentorship

One of the most widespread challenges for children's and youth ministry leaders is a lack of parental involvement and mentorship in students' faith development at home. Too often parents are comfortable (even complacent) with a diminished role in their child's spiritual maturity. Over the past fifty years or more, a growing movement of age-level worship services and fellowship groups has limited opportunities for young people to worship and minister alongside their parents. What began with a powerful vision to reach the now generation for Christ has regrettably led to a parental mind-set of outsourcing their children's spiritual discipleship only to trained pastoral leadership, the "professionals."

This "spiritual subcontracting" mind-set has inadvertently resulted in a lack of intentional discipleship at home based on the misunderstanding that their children's spirituality is sufficiently addressed at church. But in truth, once-a-week or twice-a-week sessions of two or three hours of discipleship is not enough; the teachings of the church must be reinforced at home. This lack of explicit mentorship at home—especially when paired with the inevitable inconsistencies of adults who don't always practice the ethics and values the church preaches—derails the goal of now-generation ministry, namely, the genuine transference of lifelong faith.

According to the Deuteronomy 6 passage, the primary burden of teaching children falls on the parents.[11] The ministry provided by the church to children and youth is not meant to replace mentorship provided by the parents but should work in tandem with training and discipleship already operative at home.[12] But this only highlights the underlying issue: are the parents themselves equipped with biblical knowledge and spiritually competent to mentor their children? Parents must be taught, trained, and constantly reminded that their daily Christlike example at home will be one of the greatest spiritual influences in their children's lives.

Cooperation between parents and youth ministers may begin with recalling the teachings provided in Deuteronomy 6:4-7, progress to Paul's exhortation to fathers to discipline and instruct their children in the Lord (Eph. 6:4), and mediate on the reminder in 2 Timothy 1:5 that faith is best modeled and imitated in the family: "I am reminded of your sincere faith, a faith that dwelt first in your grandmother Lois and your mother Eunice and now, I am sure, dwells in you as well" (ESV). No one will leave a deeper impression on the children's spiritual growth than parents themselves. Effective ministry to the now generation must actively seek to encourage and facilitate spiritual mentorship at home.

ANA Children's and Youth Ministry Strengths— and Weaknesses

One of the greatest advantages of serving in an ANA ministry context is the intrinsic respect for authority, especially toward pastoral and spiritual leaders. This inherent cultural respect contributes to expediting relationships of trust between students and ministers as well as that between parents and ministers. Further, due to a significant emphasis on academics and education, there is less pressure to entertain students and therefore more freedom to implement a ministry philosophy based on Bible study, memorization, and preaching.[13] Their collective support for ministry events and volunteerism are sacrificial and substantial. All of these strengths and advantages can result in very fruitful and satisfying ministry, even with limited time and financial resources.

Not surprisingly, many of the strengths and blessings of the ANA community are simultaneously its weaknesses and challenges for children's and youth ministries. For example, ANA parents support a Bible-focused and teaching-centered approach to discipleship, but often spiritual values and priorities are sidelined by academic demands and scheduling. Given the choice between Bible study and academics, the latter usually trumps the former. In addition, many ANA students struggle with self-worth based on scholastic success (or failure) and meeting the exalted expectations of a shame-based and performance-driven culture. Based on my (Sam) experience in pastoring and counseling students, there seems to be a pattern of emotional and mental distress among ANA children and youth, which is fostered by a culture that does not encourage sharing burdens, problems, and struggles.

Another weakness lies in the cultural barriers in the ANA churches. A prominent barrier is the age discrimination toward children's and youth ministry often evident in executive decisions made from senior leadership. The children's/youth ministers' opinion is not solicited, and the needs of children and youth are often marginalized by the needs of adults. And while education is highly esteemed in Asian culture, frequently the spiritual teaching of children is not as venerated as the teaching for adults. Moreover, this bias against children's/youth ministry is compounded by sexism. The cultural barrier against women does not hinder service as children's/youth ministers but poses complications in building the much-needed strong partnerships with male senior pastors. For female ministers, the difficulty of forming healthy relationships with church leadership further impedes the effort to minister effectively to children and youth.

Finally, as mentioned above, although there is high level of parental involvement on a public and communal level, ANA parents engage in very little spiritual mentorship, follow-up, and daily discipleship at home. This issue takes on a different nuance due to cultural barriers. All too often, parents are discouraged in their attempts to mentor their children because of language barriers. Communicating spiritual insight is not an easy task, but the same effort becomes intensified when the parents can only speak in broken English. Unless the children have been trained in the "mother tongue," the simple act of communication becomes a hardship for both parties, let alone communicating spiritual truth.

Language is not the only barrier; the gap between generations is well documented even in majority culture.[14] For the immigrant family, this inherent generational gap is further loaded with a cultural gap. First-generation parents expect to preserve the values and select practices of their home culture, but second- and subsequent-generation children are increasingly adapting to the values of North American majority culture. The inevitable clash between the cultures reverberates deeply in immigrant family relationships.

Are these challenges insurmountable? The language barrier is probably the easiest to resolve: either the parent or the child can learn the other language to facilitate communication. The cultural and generational gap often proves to be the more difficult. Yet the solution is not necessarily found in accommodation to either home or host culture. Parent and child alike will thrive by accommodating themselves to the culture of Scripture. By that, we do not refer to ancient Israelite or first-century Jewish or Greco-Roman cultures. Rather, the phrase "culture of Scripture" points to the essential principles necessary for a covenantal relationship with God, such as living by faith and not by works (Rom. 1:17), perseverance in the midst of strife (James 1:3), and hope for future glory (Rom. 8:24-25). This "culture of Scripture" takes precedence to both the culture of the mother land and North American culture. As both parent and child conform to Christ as Scripture mandates, the parent can model relinquishment of personal preferences to the child, and both will find the common point of contact—Christ.

Biblical and Theological Reflections for ANA Now-Generation Ministry

The above description of the current ANA children's and youth ministry, with its strengths and weaknesses, is a broad assessment of the common concerns raised in the track discussions at the ANA Consultation in May 2009. To be sure, many more variations and details can be added to our portrait. However, our task here is not merely descriptive. As the body of Christ, regardless of denominational differences, the church must seek counsel for her identity and function from Scripture, especially in this constantly changing culture.

Does Scripture provide an explicit theology for teaching children? If so, what is the rationale behind it? And is the rationale significant for the survival of the church? Is there anything wrong with providing entertainment for children and youth while the adults are occupied with worship and Bible study? Why or why not? These questions are concerned less with changing the status quo to lend more dignity to children's and youth ministry and more toward formulating a theology for those ministries. Yet, as clearly expressed in the May Consultation, the articulation of both *explicit* and *implicit* theology is necessary.[15]

How we live out our explicit theology becomes the material point; regardless of the explicit theology, the implicit theology ultimately carries the day. But the struggle to close the distance between our words and deeds is not new: "What good is it, my brothers and sisters, if you say you have faith but do not have works? Can faith save you? If a brother or sister is naked and lacks daily food, and one of you says to them, "Go in peace, keep warm and eat your fill," and yet you do not supply their bodily needs, what is the good of that? So faith by itself, if it has no works, is dead" (James 2:14-17, NRSV). As James succinctly describes, genuine faith is embodied in action; the faith prescribed throughout Scripture should not be demonstrated merely by words but also by conduct.

The Teaching Function

As noted above, the mandate to teach children is found in both Testaments and serves as the primary foundation for children's and youth ministry (Deut. 4:9; 6:7; Eph. 6:2). A closer examination of Deuteronomy 4:9-10 reveals the theological rationale behind the command. Deuteronomy 4:9 begins with a caution to Israel: "Only take care, and keep your soul diligently, lest you forget the things that your eyes have seen, and lest they depart from your heart all the days of your life." The subsequent exhortation to teach children is tied to this concern to remember God's redeeming acts in history: "Make them known to your children and your children's children."

The emphasis is not simply on continuous teaching ("your children and your children's children"), but on the content of teaching—God's saving activity ("make *them* known"). Why is remembrance of God's saving activity so critical to the teaching of children? In Deuteronomy 4:10-14, the Lord clarifies *what* Israel should teach their children: God's redemption of Israel from slavery in Egypt and the subsequent giving of the Law at Mount Sinai. The provision of the Law served to formalize God's covenant relationship with Israel

(Deut. 4:13; cf. Exod. 19:4-6) in fulfillment of God's promises to Abraham (Exod. 2:24; cf. Gen. 12:2,7; 17:7-8).

The continuation of the covenant relationship requires this: to know God's historical saving acts *is to know God*. We teach children so that the covenant relationship of knowing God, to honor and to revere God ("to fear") may be transferred to the subsequent generations. Teaching children God's actions of grace throughout history seeks to ensure their faithfulness to God and to God's ways for future generations.

Continued faithfulness is one of the key theological thrusts of Deuteronomy. In Deuteronomy, Israel stands at a critical historical juncture; they are finally ready to take possession of the land God promised (4:1). Deuteronomy 4:5 declares: "See I [Moses] have taught you statutes and rules, as the LORD my God commanded me, that you should do them in the land that you are entering to take possession of it." While faithfulness to God's commands secures God's continued blessings to his people, taking possession of the Promised Land means entering a region steeped in paganism and idolatry. The repeated exhortations "to remember" God's historical redemption and God's commands and "to teach" the children the same serve as the safeguard against the temptation to imitate other nations' practice of idolatry (see Deut. 12:29-32).[16]

The serious issues of culture clash and temptation to abandon God's way in order to adopt the lifestyle foreign to God's covenant are not confined to the historical account of Israel in Deuteronomy. These concerns are all too familiar for every church in the twenty-first century regardless of ethnicity. If our children are to be the recipients of God's covenant blessings, then we must teach them who God is, how God has acted in history, and how to live within the parameters of God's covenant. Remembering God's past faithfulness and obedience to God's commands seeks to ensure the now generation against temptation of syncretism and idolatry.

But how precisely do we fulfill this command "to teach" the children? Deuteronomy 6:4-9 provides some clues. The passage begins with the proclamation "The LORD our God, the LORD is one" (v. 4), a phrase that speaks not only to the unity of God (God is one, and therefore indivisible), but that there is only one God for Israel.[17] Based on the oneness of God, the people of God are called to love their God comprehensively: "with all your heart and with all your soul and with all your might" (v. 5). Loving God in this all-encompassing manner naturally requires God's commands to be written internally, *on the heart* (v. 6). According to the author of Hebrews, this is precisely what Jesus Christ does by fulfilling Jeremiah's prophecy: "This is the covenant that I will make with them after those days, declares the Lord: I will put my laws on their hearts, and write them on their minds" (Heb. 10:16; see Jer. 31:33).

Deuteronomy 6:7-9 continues to describe a lifestyle that embodies God's commands written on the heart: "You shall teach them diligently to your children, and shall talk of them when you sit in your house, and when you walk by the way, and when you lie down, and when you rise." The mandate "to teach" children is firmly anchored with covenant faithfulness; it is not a universal praise of teaching in general but applies specifically to teaching children God's commands. And this teaching is the organic product of having God's laws written on the heart (Deut. 6:6). If God's laws are already imprinted on the parents' hearts, then teaching their children the same occurs naturally.

Finally, this passage clarifies precisely when the teaching of children should take place—all the time. It is a way of life. There is no time when teaching God's commands to children is inappropriate; every opportunity, awake or asleep, is a teachable moment. As Peter C. Craigie notes: "The commandments were to be the subject of conversation both inside and outside the home, from the beginning of the day to the end of the day. In summary, the commandments were to permeate every sphere" of a person's life.[18] People with God's law inscribed on their hearts can do nothing else but produce God's laws, not only in speech but in conduct; it comes out through their pores.

Putting It into Practice

Practically speaking, how does this work? First, a person who has God's commands written internally will also have a hunger for

God's Word. Jesus himself specifies that a person "shall not live by bread alone, but by every word that comes from the mouth of God" (Matt. 4:4 and Luke 4:4, citing Deut. 8:3). Cognitive knowledge of God's Word is nonnegotiable for faithfulness. For both adult and child, a daily diet of Scripture reading, meditation, and prayer are absolute necessities.

This prescription is not new, yet Bible literacy in the North American church is at an all-time low. For many years, the average score in the Bible content (NT) exam for my (Sydney) incoming seminary students has been 35 out of 100.[19] And in 2010, only one out of ten students could claim the benefit of Bible study conducted by parents (at home) in spite of the fact that they have been attending church all their lives. Perhaps it is time for parents to take up the mantle and begin Bible studies at home. Perhaps it is time for children's and youth leaders to realign the focus of ministry on teaching the Word of God to the students. It is not only adults but also children who live by the Word of God.

But as the Pharisees and scribes of Jesus' day well demonstrated, knowledge of Scripture does not guarantee "righteous" living (see Matt 23:1-36; Luke 10:25-37). And as we have already noted, Deuteronomy 6:7-9 indicates that "teaching" children God's ways requires a "lifestyle" discipleship. Paul demonstrated this in his relationship with Timothy, to whom he had taught "Christ's ways" so well that the apostle was able to send his spiritual son as a clear reflection of himself (and thus of Christian discipleship). He also called the believers in Corinth to join in this discipleship: "For though you have countless guides in Christ, you do not have many fathers. For I became your father in Christ Jesus through the gospel. I urge you, then, be imitators of me. That is why I sent you Timothy, my beloved and faithful child in the Lord, to remind you of my ways in Christ, as I teach them everywhere in every church" (1 Cor. 4:15-17).

It is clear in this passage that Paul perceives his relationship with his Corinthian converts as that of parent-child. While this may appear patronizing to modern-day readers, the parent-child relationship primarily communicates responsibility of the parent in first-century Greco-Roman culture as well as the Jewish culture. The parent is *obligated* to the child to provide a model for imitation.[20] Again, the teaching model is both explicit and implicit, as Paul provides explicit teaching and instruction throughout this letter and also puts forth his own lifestyle for imitation.

To what degree are modern-day Christian parents able to provide their own lifestyles as models of Christ's ways to their children? How might children's and youth ministers provide themselves as models for their students? How can the senior church leadership do so? The transference of genuine faith can only take place through such models.

Living Out the Mind-set of the "Body"

One of the dominant issues discussed in the track discussions in the May Consultation was the individualistic character of children's and youth ministry. As stated earlier, the minister in charge of students is often isolated from the wider ministry of the church. Being frequently exempted from regular meetings with the church leadership, the children's or youth minister may be missing out on healthy mentoring relationships with the senior pastor and lay leadership.[21] The exclusion can be partially attributed to the cultural tendency to perceive children as secondary "citizens" and the youth workers as simply "child minders." After all, if now-generation ministers are little more than babysitters or recreational directors, then no collaborative effort is needed. But as we have already established, such a second-class view of ministry with children and youth cannot be supported biblically.

What's more, Paul's use of the body metaphor in Ephesians 4:11-16 precludes any lone-ranger mind-set in ministry. Paul envisions collaborative faithfulness via diverse functions but one identity as "the body of Christ." The various gifts are provided by Christ so that the body of Christ might be built up and the saints might be equipped (vv. 11-12). This suggests that all leaders are to work together to equip the laity and one another—and student ministries are not exempt. Not only are their leaders to play a critical role in "equipping the saints" ages twenty-five years and younger, but the children's and youth ministers themselves need to be the recipients of "equipping" and "building up" from the parents and church leadership.

According to Ephesians 4:13, mutual edification leads to "maturity in Christ" for the entire body. And maturity in Christ is explained further as unity in faith and unity in the knowledge of the Son of God. It is difficult to stand in unity of faith and the knowledge of Jesus Christ if the student minister stands alone. And as already observed in Deuteronomy 4 and 6, faith is not only for adults but must include the children as well to ensure survival. How significant is the children's/youth minister if children are the key for continuation of God's blessings? These ministers are in need of encouragement and discipleship along with the wider pastoral and lay leadership.

It's interesting to note that Paul uses the metaphor of "children" to describe those who are easily led astray by false teachings (Eph. 4:14). It is only the spiritually mature who are equipped to withstand deceitful doctrine. This is particularly insightful for us. If children are more easily deceived, then how much more should we be concerned not only with the children themselves but with the nurture and mentoring of those who minister to our young people? If children's/youth ministry is to grow and work effectively, then it must be incorporated into the overall church leadership and the laity—so that we might equip and build up one another through the Spirit's gifts and so that we stand united in faith and in the knowledge of Jesus. We are in this work together, and only through such comprehensive unity may we promote growth of the body and proper functioning of each member and ministry (v. 15).

Humility in Service

A word is needed concerning the mind-set necessary for unity. Both Jesus and Paul emphasize the one necessary ingredient for discipleship: servanthood. Often, individualistic ministry mind-set trumps cooperation due to misinterpretation of power and authority. Perhaps many internal staff disputes may be overcome through remembrance of this essential mind-set.

In Mark 10:44, Jesus tells his disciples, "Whoever would be first among you must be slave of all." This familiar verse takes on weightier significance given the context—immediately after James and John request the most honored seats next to Jesus. The object of their desire is not simply honor but power. The metaphor "to sit on the right hand" is often used in both Testaments to describe a place of power and authority.[22] (This interpretation is fortified by the phrase "in your glory" in 10:37, which also indicates the aspect of Jesus' kingdom that the brothers desire most intensely.) When the rest of the disciples learn of this privately made request, they aren't indignant about the request itself but about the power play—that the brothers beat everyone else to the bat (10:41). It is in this context that Jesus teaches the disciples that the servant mind-set is the greatest and most honored position in the kingdom of God.[23]

Whether the disciples understood Jesus' lesson is unclear, but the more material question is, have *we* understood it? How would this servant mind-set affect the internal relations of church leadership and the laity in the ANA church, and particularly among ministry leaders such as the now-generation ministers? We must aim not simply for unity under any flag, but that of the Christ crucified, who embodied the servant disposition. Remember Philippians 2:1-11, where Paul urged the believers to look to the interests of others (v. 4) and to honor the other as being more significant than the self (v. 3).

The same lesson is illustrated powerfully in John 13, where Jesus adopts the actions of a slave and washes his disciples' feet. He explicitly commands his disciples to follow his example:

> Do you understand what I have done to you? You call me Teacher and Lord, and you are right, for so I am. If then I, your Lord and Teacher, have washed your feet, you also ought to wash one another's feet. For I have given you an example, that you also should do just as I have done to you. Truly, truly, I say to you, a servant is not greater than his master, nor is a messenger greater than the one who sent him. If you know these things, blessed are you if you do them. (vv. 12-17)

Christ's life and Paul's teachings agree: leadership is not a demonstration of dominion or power. The disposition of a Christian disciple reflects humility and a love that leads to honoring and serving the other. This principle informs how senior leadership value now-generation ministers, and it also humbles any tendency of younger leaders to dismiss senior leadership as "outdated" or "ineffective." Such attitudes lead not only to severed communication and broken relations but also foster insubordination and violate the essential requirement of "submitting to one another" (Eph. 5:21).

What does this have to do with effective children's and youth ministry? The humble disposition of all church leadership, pastoral and lay, teaches children and youth by example how to live out the explicit teaching of Scripture. Apart from this paradigm of humility and service in leadership, all efforts to teach children about God's commands and a gospel of grace are in vain.

God Puts a Comma Where We Put a Period

One of my (Sam) former youth ministry students (who attended Virginia Tech and was on campus during the shooting) seemed to be destined to be another "statistic" of students who gradually fall away from the church and/or God. During the middle of her senior year of high school, she confided in me how she became disillusioned, disheartened, and disconnected with our local church and faith community. Even though she stopped attending our church before she graduated, I kept in touch with her throughout her college career via email and during holiday and semester breaks. I still had tremendous optimism and hope for her spiritual life because she was surrounded by parents and siblings who unconditionally loved her and incessantly prayed for her walk with God.

Despite how her spiritual life ended during the high school years, I was encouraged to hear that she had continued to grow in her faith by plugging into a solid campus fellowship, actively attending a local church, and dating a devoted follower of Christ. During her first semester of her senior year in college, she shared with me that she and her Christian boyfriend had gotten engaged. I couldn't have been more thrilled. A few months before their wedding, she and her fiancée joined my wife and me for dinner at our home. I was really blessed and encouraged by their relationship with one another and desire to follow after God. Then she asked me to officiate their wedding at my church, the same church she grew up in and the same church she rejected during her high school years, but one her parents continued to attend. It was an invitation I couldn't refuse!

Through this student's testimony, I am reminded that as we boldly raise up and passionately "pass the torch" to the now generation, we must remain humble to how and when God operates and touches people's lives. It is only by grace that we are saved. And it is only by God's grace that we can serve and seek to build the kingdom one genuine smile, one gentle conversation, one bold prayer, and one child at a time.

✦

NOTES

1. Ian Shapira and Tom Jackman, "Gunman Kills 32 at Virginia Tech in Deadliest Shooting in U.S. History," *Washington Post*, April 17, www.washingtonpost.com/wp-dyn/content/article/2007/04/16/AR2007041600533.html.

2. Amy Gardner and David Cho, "Isolation Defined Cho's Senior Year," *Washington Post*, May 6, 2007, www.washingtonpost.com/wp-dyn/content/article/2007/05/05/AR2007050501221.html.

3. See Christian Smith, *Soul Searching: The Religious and Spiritual Lives of American Teenagers* (Oxford: Oxford University Press, 2005), 3–8, for an insightful analysis of modern-day challenges for teenagers and parents in America.

4. See Mark H. Senter III, Wesley Black, Chap Clark, and Malan Nel, *Four Views of Youth Ministry and the Church* (Grand Rapids: Zondervan, 2001). In spite of distinct emphases of the four perspectives, they virtually all agree on one point: children's/youth ministry must be perceived as an essential component of the church requiring involvement from all levels of the church. See also Fernando Arzola Jr., "The Holistic Approach," in *Toward a Prophetic Youth Ministry: Theory and Praxis in Urban Context* (Downers Grove, IL: IVP Academic, 2008), 44–53.

5. In particular, see Black, "The Preparatory Approach to Youth Ministry," in *Four Views*, 39–60, for emphasis on the need for a comprehensive approach to children's and youth ministry.

6. See Sam O'Neal, "Youth Ministry Gets Serious," *Christianity Today*, January 1, 2007.

7. Kara Powell, "Is the Era of Age Segregation Over?" *Leadership Journal,* Summer 2009, 43–45.

8. Mark DeVries, *Sustainable Youth Ministry* (Downers Grove, IL: InterVarsity, 2008), 126, citing a statistical study, provides wise counsel on this issue: "Persevere. The longer you minister with youth, the more goals you will see accomplished, the more competent and confident you will feel, the more satisfaction you will derive from your relationships with youth and their parents and the stronger will be your sense of purpose and confidence in God and his Word."

9. See Senter, "The Strategic Approach to Youth Ministry," in *Four Views*, 114–35. He says, "Youth pastors must be viewed as pastors" and stipulates not only strict requirements for selection and development of youth ministers, but also the necessity of entrusting to them full authority of pastors (132).

10. Ibid., 114–15. Senter provides an apt illustration of a church's failure only perceived when a ten-year reunion of their youth group yielded less than half of the original youth group. He isolates two core issues for this failure: marginalization of the youth and discontinuity in spiritual nurture.

11. Tricia Graves, "Pragmatic-Participatory Model," in *Perspectives on Children's Spiritual Formation: Four Views*, ed. M. J. Anthony (Nashville: B & H Academic, 2006) 165–206. Based on her examination of Old Testament passages, Graves identifies the parents as the primary source for children's spiritual nurture and training (168).

12. Ibid., 169.

13. According to O'Neal, "Youth Ministry Gets Serious," the youth's hunger for a stronger emphasis on teaching seems to transcend ethnic boundaries: "To reverse the trend, *Time* reports some churches are focusing more on teaching. Ben Calmer vetoed the purchase of a pool table after he became youth pastor of Shoreline Christian Center in Austin, Texas. The teens don't seem to miss the entertainment, as attendance doubled to 160 in the 18 months Calmer has been on the job."

14. See Peter Cha, Paul Kim, and Dihan Lee, "Multigenerational Households," in *Growing Healthy Asian American Churches: Ministry Insights from Groundbreaking Congregations*, ed. Peter Cha, S. Steve Kang, and Helen Lee (Downers Grove, IL: InterVarsity, 2006), 145–63.

15. Graves, "Pragmatic," 172, states something similar: "God challenges parents to be engaged in communicating God's truth both formally and informally and both in conversation and visually. Many spiritual lessons are taught through interaction between parents and their children outside the context of a formal church or classroom setting."

16. See Paul R. House, *Old Testament Theology* (Downers Grove, IL: InterVarsity, 1998), 182–84.

17. J. Gordon McConville, *Deuteronomy*, Apollos Old Testament Commentary Series, vol. 5 (Downers Grove, IL: InterVarsity, 2002), 140–41.

18. Peter C. Craigie, *The Book of Deuteronomy*, The New International Commentary on the Old Testament (Grand Rapids: Eerdmans, 1976), 170.

19. For similar assessment, see David R. Nienhuis, "The Problem of Evangelical Biblical Illiteracy: A View from the Classroom," *Modern Reformation* 19, no. 1 (January/February 2010): 10–13, 17. Nienhuis insightfully notes that the issue goes beyond simple ability to recall biblical data. The dilemma lies in their ignorance of the basic biblical narrative.

20. Andrew D. Clarke, *Serve the Community of the Church: Christians as Leaders and Ministers* (Grand Rapids: Eerdmans, 2000), 90–92; see also Richard P. Saller, *Patriarchy, Property and Death in the Roman Family* (Cambridge: Cambridge University Press, 1994), 111–12.

21. The ineffective dynamics between senior and youth pastor is not isolated to ANA churches. Irrespective of ethnic diversity, this relationship is critical to the success of children's and youth ministry within the church. DeVries, *Sustainable Youth Ministry*, 13, quotes R. King, "The cycle of dysfunctional relationships between senior pastors and youth pastors must be broken. Youth pastors must learn how to commit themselves to uniquely prioritizing this relationship."

22. See Deuteronomy 33:2; Psalm 16:8; 109:31; 110:1,5; Matthew 22:44 (para. Mark 12:36; Luke 20:42; Acts 2:34; Heb. 1:13) citing Psalm 110:1; Matthew 26:64 (para. Mark 14:62; Luke 22:69); Mark 16:19; Acts 2:25 citing Psalm 16:8; Acts 7:55–56. See also C. A. Evans, *Mark 8:27–16:20*, Word Biblical Commentary (Nashville: Thomas Nelson, 2001), 116.

23. The word *doulos* in verse 44 is translated "servant" in most translations but means "slave."

PART TWO

✝

MINISTRY ISSUES

CHAPTER 5

✝

Forming "Grace-Full" Pastors

PETER T. CHA AND
GREG J. YEE

"Pastor Wayne, I know God is calling me to a vocation of ministry, but I know that I'm not called to serve as a pastor of a local church," said the college senior as he sipped his coffee. "I want to serve in a place where God's Spirit is actively at work, not in a local church where people only seem to get hurt and don't grow." These were the final words Pastor Wayne heard from Kenny as they wrapped up their summer-long spiritual mentoring relationship.[1]

Late that afternoon, alone in his office, Pastor Wayne reflected on and wrestled with Kenny's parting words. Personally, he felt disappointed and even rejected by the young leader of his church's college group. Knowing Kenny's strong desire to serve God and recognizing that he had many exceptional qualities that should make him a wonderful pastor, Pastor Wayne met with him weekly to mentor him and to introduce him to the world of pastoral ministry. That morning's conversation clearly revealed that Kenny had no interest in even entertaining the possibility that God might be calling him to be a local church pastor.

"Times have changed," Pastor Wayne told himself as he reminisced about the significant conversation he had had with his own pastor more than twenty years ago. Wayne had been a college sophomore when the pastor of his immigrant church took him aside one day and challenged him to pray earnestly about what might be God's calling for him. The aging pastor had then added, "I have been watching you closely since your youth group years. I would not be surprised if God is calling you to pastoral ministry." Pastor Wayne remembered how the unsolicited remark had both surprised and affirmed him, and how that short exchange began to fill his mind and heart with a desire to serve in a church like the one that had played such a significant role in the spiritual growth of his entire family.

How different Kenny's response was from what his own had been. "What does this say about how our young people experience church today and how they view pastoral ministry?" asked Pastor Wayne as he was getting ready to leave his office. Then came even more unsettling questions: "Do the ministry of this church and my pastoral ministry show any signs of God's transformative power and grace? Can I fault Kenny for not seeing much hope in this place? Why *would* anyone as gifted as Kenny aspire to be the pastor of a dysfunctional church like this one?"

The Challenge of Today's Pastoral Ministry

We are all too familiar with stories of embarrassing displays of good Christian people thinking and acting unchristianly. The household of God is described by aberrant displays of judgmental, aggressive, and ungracious church people. These incidents can be painfully public, especially when the conflict involves pastors and their families, and the result is a shadowy alter ego to the bride of Christ. Paul boldly proclaimed the power we have in Christ to do immeasurably more than we could even think to ask or have depth to imagine (Eph. 3:20-21), but too often another power seems to be at work in our churches.

When congregational conflict and strife occur, pastors and their families often experience the anguish in isolation and enforced silence. But the effects of this lonely experience are like a silent scream. Organizations that dedicate themselves to the care and counsel of church leaders, such as the Leader Renewal Institute, document these effects both statistically and anecdotally. Reports from several of these organizations agree on the epidemic rates of pastoral burnout, decreasing self-esteem, and the negative impact on clergy families. Each month 1,200 pastors are forced to leave their positions, and fully half of full-time pastors leave ministry within the first five years.[2]

The details continue to emerge. For example, the Evangelical Lutheran Church of America (ELCA) recently conducted a comprehensive study on clergy health that yielded alarming results. Clergy are found to have higher levels of obesity, stress, and behavioral health admissions. The top five classes of drugs prescribed to pastors were for high cholesterol, depression, ulcers, inflammation or pain, and high blood pressure.[3] One striking statistic is that, in the 1950s Protestant clergy lived longer than other males. By the 1990s, however, being a pastor meant being counted among the ten most likely professions to suffer heart disease.[4]

One study done on clergy burnout by William Grosch and David Olsen raises the question of why clergy, who "begin their careers with high idealism, optimism, and compassion," face such negative results in their ministries. They recognize two major sources of burnout. The first stems from "external systemic factors," including paralyzing bureaucracy, poor administrative support, and difficult work conditions. The second stems from "intrapersonal factors" such as "high idealism, Type-A personality, narcissism, and perfectionism."[5]

These overall challenges for pastoral ministry may be exacerbated in the ANA context where the struggle to handle the "external systemic factors" becomes a common and familiar experience. There are patterns of unhealthy communication between leaders and unbiblical nonconfrontational approaches to conflict resolution. Passive aggressive tendencies by senior pastoral staff escalate relational tensions, which often explode on junior staff members. Pastors are expected to perform excellently without mentoring or encouragement. They are expected to work seventy- to eighty-hour workweeks at the expense of self and family.

Within the Asian shame-based culture, there is little space to fail, and within a strict hierarchy, there is little to no room for collaboration or collective discernment. This often reinforces the marginalizing of younger leaders. Pastors quickly learn that if they are going to survive they must ignore these challenges and "just be faithful." These external and systemic issues layer themselves on intrapersonal factors—challenges such as being a "people pleaser," a perfectionist, or overly driven come together to create a potentially lethal combination. Not surprisingly, the *Pulpit & Pew: Asian American Religious Leadership Today* describes the "most acute tensions" in Asian American churches as being in the area of generational clashes concerning philosophy of ministry and concerning the overall negative ethos and practice within churches (as we have described above).[6]

On an equally frightening front, we must heed signs that we see emerging within seminaries as well. Because of the challenging conditions in so many churches and in ANA congregations in particular, the draw to enter into vocational ministry has become less attractive. Along with high attrition rates among local church clergy, there are decreasing rates of enrollment in MDiv programs. After decades of rapid growth, the Association of Theological Schools (ATS) is now reporting that Asian student enrollment has stopped growing in recent years.[7] We saw these signs growing years ago, when a 2007 *Los Angeles Times* article ran the headline "Asian American Churches Face Leadership Gap—Pastors Aren't Being Prepared to Handle Congregational Conflicts over Cultural and Generational Issues." In this article, a national summit of directors of seminary-based Asian American Christian centers warned of this "crisis of leadership."[8]

Biblical and Theological Reflections on Pastoral Formation and Ministry

The trajectory of ANA churches testifies to a lack of prioritization to develop and form young healthy missional leaders. We are at a critical moment. Our population is booming. The 2006 Canadian Census and 2010 US Census report that Asians continue to hold the fastest-growing percentage among ethnic groups. We see immediate challenges and now grow increasingly concerned for the exploding population and emerging generations that inherit this deficit. We are at a crossroads and must determine our first steps out of the cycles of cultural and ecclesiastical dysfunction.

What would a healthy ANA pastoral ministry look like? In what ways do ANA congregations and pastors need to reframe their understanding of the nature and role of pastors so that pastors can faithfully and effectively serve God and God's church? During the 2009 consultation, fourteen ANA pastors, theologians, and seminarians engaged with these questions in the track on pastoral formation. Examining various challenges ANA ministries face, as well as the nature and role of the church as described in Ephesians, these participants collaboratively reflected on the theme of pastoral identity (i.e., who pastors are called to be). If the church is indeed a household of God, what role does the pastor serve in that setting? More specifically, if the ANA church is to grow as a healthy family of God, what kind of pastor is needed?

Pastor as Christ Follower

In ANA families and organizations, we are often defined by the roles we play in the group.[9] As the firstborn son of the family, I (Peter) learned early on that I had a particular role to play in my large family. As I sought to help my immigrant parents navigate the unfamiliar landscape of American culture and to mediate between my parents and my five younger brothers and sisters, I was awarded with an identity that became important to me: I was a "good number one son." Years later, when I became a pastor of an English Ministry (EM) congregation within the immigrant church, I implicitly understood that the role I was to play in this church was quite similar to the one I had played all along in my own family—be a "good number one son." In the ANA's collectivistic culture, the particular services you provide and the duties you perform for the good of the group significantly define who you are.

In Ephesians, the apostle Paul gives some attention to the roles and responsibilities that different leaders and members of the church need to play, including those who are called to serve as pastor-teachers. He writes, "So Christ himself gave the apostles, the prophets, the evangelists, the pastors and teachers, to equip his people for works of service, so that the body of Christ may be built up" (4:11-12, NIV). These and other instructions offer significant biblical insights regarding the nature and purpose of pastoral ministry. However, it is important to note that in Ephesians and elsewhere, Paul makes a distinction between the roles we play in the church and our identity as Christians, that they are not to be fused as they often appear to be in ANA settings, including churches.

More than that, Paul declares that our identity precedes the roles we are assigned to play, that our roles and duties flow out of the reality of who we are, our identity in Christ. According to Ephesians, we are first the children of God (1:5) who were adopted into God's household and became the recipients of God's saving grace (2:8). In short, before we are called to be pastors, we are first called by our gracious God to be beloved children, God's own redeemed people who are followers of Christ. Today's ANA churches and pastors need to reclaim this simple but often overlooked truth.

What does this mean in terms of how we view and approach what pastoral ministry is, particularly in today's ANA congregational settings? First, pastors need to embrace and emphasize their shared identity with their congregational members, that all are "saved-by-grace" Christ followers. Today in some ANA churches, pastors often feel like "hired hands" of the church, employed to fulfill a set of contractual duties, rather than fellow members of the same household of God. On the other hand, in some church settings, pastors are treated as if they belong to an elite spiritual caste, today's superapostles who can lead churches to the Promised Land, meeting all their needs and expectations along the way. In either scenario, pastors are perceived as "others" who do not belong to the household of God in the same way that the lay members do. The Ephesians' theology of church, however, does not allow room for such divisions in God's family. "There is one body and one Spirit . . . one Lord, one faith, one baptism, one God and Father of all" (Eph.

4:4-6, ESV), declares Paul. In the household of one Father, there cannot be "us" and "them"—there is only "us."

Second, if the core of pastoral identity is the "saved by grace" Christ follower, our understanding of what we do as pastors must be informed by this identity as well. The apostle Paul both modeled and taught that we can serve God's church first and foremost by being a faithful follower of Christ. In writing his epistle to the Philippians, one of Paul's central pastoral concerns was the threat of disunity and conflicts in the church.[10] However, before he performs his pastoral duty of restoring unity in the church, Paul first reminds them of their shared identity as Christ followers, urging others to continue to journey with him in following Christ.

A few years ago, I (Peter) assigned a book called *The Art of Pastoring: Ministry without All the Answers* in one of my pastoral theology courses at Trinity Evangelical Divinity School. In this book, David Hansen, a Baptist pastor who served two rural congregations in Montana, argued persuasively that the main, if not only, "job description" of a pastor is to be a faithful and winsome Christ follower. He writes, "I have discovered that when I follow Jesus in my everyday life as a pastor, people meet Jesus through my life."[11] So, as Jesus had done, Pastor Hansen spends much time with people in their own settings, with both believers and nonbelievers. An avid lover of fly-fishing, this pastor of two churches regularly finds time to go fly-fishing, often inviting others to come along, to enjoy God's creation and to reflect on God's goodness.

Most students in the class expressed their appreciation for this pastor's simple but profound approach to pastoral ministry because it is so contrary to other books on pastoral ministry that promote the latest ministry trends, methods, and tasks. However, the students who were impacted most profoundly by this book were ANA seminarians in the class. These young men and women were drawn to this simple picture of pastoral ministry even more because they come from a culture and church that strongly emphasize performance and achievement. Precisely because of these cultural and social values, they acknowledged that the pastoral ministry portrayed by David Hansen is an ideal that cannot be experienced in most ANA churches. In short, "pastor as a Christ follower" calls for significant reframing of both ANA pastors' and congregations' understanding of who they are.

Pastor as Wounded Healer

Today there are two basic types of churches. The first is one that functions like an art museum and the second, a hospital. Church is like an art museum when it becomes a place where people gather to display their (and their children's) economic and social achievements. In contrast, church is like a hospital when it becomes a gathering place of those who recognize that they are not well and seek healing. Given certain ANA values (e.g., educational achievements) and tendencies (e.g., strong work ethic and perfectionism), ANA churches can too easily become like art museums. Yet it is clear that the church Paul envisions in Ephesians is that of grace, healing, and service, a place that is more like a hospital.

If the household of God were to become a place of healing and wellness—of *shalom*—a reality that is too infrequently experienced in many ANA churches, what particular role should a pastor play in the process? Our Lord Jesus is the Master Physician who not only provided healing to many but also commissioned his disciples to engage in kingdom ministry, which included healing the sick in his name (Matt. 10:5-8). This same Lord, who is the head of our church, still desires to bring much-needed healing to his church, the household of God—and Jesus is calling his followers, including pastors, to participate in this ministry of healing in his name. However, lest we become prideful, the Scriptures continually remind us that we all are sinners who are saved only through grace. We are not the source of healing; we are merely the conduits of God's healing. In fact, it is often in and through our own pain and weakness that God does his mighty work of healing.

In his classic work *The Wounded Healer*, Henri Nouwen made a compelling argument that those who are entering into ministry need to see themselves as "wounded healers."[12] He noted that in a fragmented world that is filled with rapid change and suffering, a minister cannot simply follow the guidelines offered by a "handbook for ministers" or other types of "how-to" manuals. Rather, an essential part of one's ministry in a broken world is to be in touch with one's own woundedness as well as that of others, and of our world.

This theme of pastor as "wounded healer" is even more critical when it comes to the ministry of reconciliation, of peacemaking. As indicated earlier in this chapter, one of the significant challenges many ANA churches face is ongoing conflict among its members and leaders. As pastors, an important part of our ministry is to serve as peacemakers, making it necessary for us to continue to grow in our skills and abilities to become more effective in this important role. However, the ministry of reconciliation might look a little different if it were to be facilitated by a pastor who sees himself or herself as a wounded healer, not simply a skilled negotiator.

A wounded healer who understands God's saving grace takes both sides first to the foot of the cross as the apostle Paul does in Ephesians 2, not just to the negotiating table. Paul reminds God's people that on the cross not only were each individual's sins wiped away but people's hostilities toward "others" were put to death as well (v. 16). When we have hostility toward our brothers and sisters in the household of God, we not only sin against those individuals but against God and our Savior himself, a sin that calls for both individual and corporate repentance.

In 1907 a powerful revival broke out in Pyongyang, today's capital city of North Korea, and spread throughout the rest of the country during the following several years. This revival took place at an annual, ten-day Bible conference where 1,500 Western missionaries and Korean pastors gathered. During one session, prompted by the Holy Spirit, many Korean Christian leaders and Western missionaries began to confess their sins before one another. Many missionaries confessed their racism toward the Korean believers, while many Korean pastors and elders publicly acknowledged feelings of hostility toward the Western missionaries. This practice continued for a whole week, allowing God's people to experience God's healing grace and power and allowing missionaries and Korean believers to work together in unity, as one household of God.[13]

This powerful example from Asia reminds us that the foot of the cross is a very transformative space for God's divine work of reconciliation and peacemaking, for the crucified Savior himself is our peace (Eph. 2:14). This Savior of peace invites today's ANA pastors to bring their congregations to this sacred place, especially when they are experiencing relational conflicts and breakdowns. However, pastors are not to come along as guides or teachers but as wounded healers, as Korean pastors and missionaries had done more than a century ago. Such reconciliation leads to true repentance that, in turn, invites the whole congregation to experience yet once again that we are truly saved and revived by God's grace alone (vv. 8-10).

Pastor as Rebuilder

I (Greg) was in the parking lot at Candlestick Park on October 17, 1989, in San Francisco. As I walked toward the stadium, the 6.9 magnitude "World Series Quake" struck the Bay Area and Santa Cruz, killing 63, injuring 3,757, leaving up to 12,000 homeless, and stranding me on the wrong side of the bay from my home in Oakland. My work with the San Francisco Conservation Corps at that time allowed me to see how lives were changed forever. Damage was estimated at $6 billion. I had to change my own patterns and expectations as transportation became more complicated with the bay's busiest bridge closed down.

For Californians, earthquakes happen. Some are small, and others are like the quake of '89. But they are a part of life. Likewise, for church leaders, conflict happens. There are everyday conflicts and there are painfully large ones. We need to understand that it is not a matter of *if* you will have them; it is *how intense* you will have them. Our call to suffer as followers of Christ assumes conflict (Luke 14:25-33; Rom. 12:17-21; Phil. 1:29-30). We must change our natural and cultural inclinations to avoid conflict. Part of being a rebuilder during times of church earthquakes is jumping right into the epicenter of the messy and painful relational work. We need to embrace conflict and see it as a necessary part of continuing to build the household of God. Two principles of church conflict management need to be highlighted here.

1. *Know the Value of Conflict.* M. Scott Peck's model for community making tells us that knowing conflict's value is a nonnegotiable. His model progresses from a level of pseudo-community (surface depth), to chaos (dealing with real issues), to surrender (compromise and loving well), to genuine community.[14] Peck reminds us that part of being the household of God is that it is made up of diverse people with different personalities, family backgrounds, communication patterns, cultures, stages, etc. The household of God brings together that which was hostile and different and brings it peacefully together to be *one* (Eph. 2:14; 4:2-6). This does not mean that we somehow magically assimilate into some collective when we become Christians. We remain unique even when we come together in Christ's body.

Conflict brings a sense of chaos; intense conflict brings an intense sense of chaos. At this point, we either retreat to pseudo-community where we settle for mere surface-level interactions, or we roll up our sleeves and learn to push through the chaos. When we choose the latter, we then must enter the stage of learning to surrender the right of winning it all. It is an exercise in listening well, offering compromise, and making decisions to love well (1 Cor. 13:4-8). We can have *faith* that things might get better. We can *hope* that things will turn around. We certainly believe that the greatest thing is *loving* well. What more intense time can we have to express love than when we are in conflict? We need conflict and chaos to shape and mature us, and ironically to unify us.

2. *Have Clear Expectations.* In my role, I (Greg) am regularly called into conflictual church situations to help. I have found that there are two types of churches when it comes to dealing with conflict—those that have unclear expectations and those that overtly spell out their expectations.

Churches with unclear expectations may randomly teach on reconciliation and forgiveness, but they will seldom create a culture of it. Principles of confrontation (Matt. 18:15-20) and principles of living with conflict (Rom. 12:17-21) disappear in the cloud of pain and hurt when things go wrong. We settle for a "nicey-nice" Christian veneer and pretend that being the church is about avoiding conflict. Our Asian culture tends to perceive conflict as wrong and something to be avoided. One extreme perspective is that conflict is actually sin.

Other churches are more deliberate. Some will explicitly state biblical principles of how people are to be treated in their core values. Some will clearly teach what is expected in their membership classes and ask people to sign an agreement. These are churches that clearly understand that conflict is natural and normal, and the emphasis is on *how* to go through it.

In the ANA context, explicit instructions and expectations can be an effective strategy to overcome natural cultural cues concerning conflict. Intentional modeling by pastoral staff and leaders can reshape unhealthy family and church patterns. Ministry heads and small group leaders are well positioned in the front lines to break the cycles of avoidance and shame associated with conflict. They are vitally placed to help begin recasting an atmosphere of grace, peace, and wholeness. *Shalom* is realized in these basic relationships of a church family. From there, *shalom* naturally moves outward.

A new culture begins to take root. When roots grow stronger and run deeper, spring always brings greater fruitfulness. Christ leads us forward, inviting us to be a contagious fragrance to a broken world (2 Cor. 2:14-16). The power of a community that deals with conflict becomes a more credible witness. New life and renewed relationships directly correlate to missional effectiveness. It also follows that members who regularly see and taste biblical reconciliation will be attuned instinctually to see where reconciliation is needed around them in the community, city, and world.

Toward Becoming Grace-full Pastors

As the Bay Area emerged out of the initial shock from the earthquake, the natural next step was to rebuild. Some things could be rebuilt to their original state. Most things were rebuilt into a stronger state. Some things had to be removed altogether. One of the greatest tasks of a rebuilder is to determine the extent of the rebuilding process. What needs to be rebuilt to its original state? In the church, it is perhaps a sense of family and a recommitment to being together. What needs to be rebuilt stronger? Perhaps it is how communication happens. What needs to be removed altogether? Perhaps there are cultural norms that have been trumping biblical values. Perhaps there are church norms that stifle honest engagement with each other.

It is God's intentions for the church to be about rebuilding. God's intent was that "through the church the manifold wisdom of God might now be made known to the rulers and authorities in the heavenly places. This was according to the eternal purpose that he has realized in Christ Jesus our Lord" (Eph. 3:10-11, ESV). It is the church that gives testimony to the spirit world of the reconciling work of Christ on the cross. We as pastors are called to help lead this rebuilding work in the church.

What then are some concrete steps that can help ANA congregations grow as healthy households of God's people? In what ways can today's ANA churches and pastors live out the biblical principles outlined in the previous section so that pastors can faithfully carry out their ministry responsibilities without getting burned out? How can today's churches contribute toward the formation of pastors who see themselves as Christ followers, wounded healers, and rebuilders?

Restoring the Biblical Image of the Church

In *The Essence of the Church*, Craig Van Gelder argues that many churches in North America experience much confusion because they have a distorted picture of what the church is.[15] In particular, many North American churches see themselves as "voluntary associations," organizations that consist of members who choose to belong simply because their particular needs are being met.[16] Furthermore, in a consumeristic culture where public institutions feel compelled to "brand" themselves in order to recruit new "customers,"[17] churches are increasingly adopting various marketing strategies and principles.[18] These practices—and values that emerge from them—gradually shape the church's self-understanding of what it is, a "spiritual marketplace" whose main mission is to attract new customers by offering new and better programs. In such a setting, congregation members identify themselves as savvy spiritual consumers who often voice their own needs, pressuring church leaders to deliver certain goods. Church pastors, in turn, feel the mounting pressure to strive for entrepreneurial excellence in order to hold on to their own members while attracting new members.

ANA congregations and pastors are not shielded from this powerful sociological force. Given the strong values of performance and achievement in ANA cultures, this tendency is reinforced further in these congregations, thus putting more pressure on ANA pastors to do more and better. This notion of church as a "spiritual marketplace" also contributes to various frictions and conflicts within churches since different groups demand different, and often competing, priorities. However, what if the ANA church intentionally moves away from the mind-set of seeing itself as a "spiritual marketplace" and begins to see itself as a household of God's people? What if ANA church members do not see themselves as fickle and demanding consumers but as individuals who have been graciously adopted into a new family? What if ANA pastors do not see themselves as marketing directors who sell certain products but as fellow members of the family to whom certain responsibilities of leadership are given?

During the 2009 consultation process, many ANA pastors voiced that the formation of healthy pastors and congregational ministries in the ANA church needs to begin with the church's reclaiming of the biblical picture of what a church is.[19] So how does a congregation go about appropriating a biblical understanding of the nature of the church and reflecting on its implications?

The participants in the pastoral formation track agreed that this process of reframing must begin with a sustained reflection on God's Word. The process invites the congregation and the pastor together to listen to God by digging deeper into the Scriptures. At the same time, it also needs to involve some type of group in which all have an opportunity to contribute their voices. Both are needed. However, while most churches are very familiar with the former, not many experience the latter method of group reflections and interaction.

Let us recommend a group exercise that the 2009 consultation used.[20] Begin the exercise by distributing a large blank note card to each participant. Then invite all participants, by reflecting on the teaching and their congregational experiences, to come up with one word that best captures the picture of what church is or ought to be. Next, request participants to write the word on their cards and bring them to the front of the room and tape them on the wall. As they do so, encourage them to look at other words that are posted and place their cards close to others that share similar ideas or themes. When all the note cards are posted, after offering some time to study what is on the wall, invite the group to help the facilitator to move certain words around so that emerging themes can become further strengthened and some connections between different themes can be established.

What might eventually emerge is the group's shared understanding and vision of what church is or can be. When the pastoral formation consultation track conducted this exercise, the following were some key themes that emerged: grace-filled, reconciled, wounded healer, transformational, gospel-driven, Christ-centered, healthy, and expanding household. Having these word pictures, then, enabled the consultation participants to focus specifically on the nature and role of pastoral ministry in such a congregational setting, producing insights that contributed to the writing of this chapter.

Reframing the Image of the Pastor

Today there are many pastors' conferences that portray pastors as CEOs of complex organizations, leaders who must be able to cast a compelling vision and develop and implement long-range plans while managing well the paid and volunteer staff members. Given that many churches function as a "spiritual marketplace," the pervasiveness of this image of the pastor is an understandable sociological phenomenon. However, if the church is more like a family, a household of God, the pastor needs to reframe his or her own understanding of the nature of the vocation, as this chapter asserts. But when and how should such a process of reframing take place?

In 2007 the Catalyst Leadership Center[21] started an eighteen-month-long pastoral mentoring program for young ANA pastors in the East Coast area. Named Scrubs,[22] this program was organized around the theme of "brokenness," exploring (1) our own brokenness as pastors, (2) the brokenness of our congregations, and (3) the brokenness of our lost world. Some Catalyst board members wondered if busy young pastors would commit to participating in this relatively lengthy program since it did not promise a new set of leadership skills or a sizable ministry toolbox. However, twelve young pastors and six mentors had rich experiences of healing and grace.

In the three modules (each met for three days), the size and numerical growth of our congregations or various successes in our ministry programs were topics conspicuously absent from our conversation. Rather, we focused on our own brokenness before God and our desperate need of God's grace and of support from colleagues in the community.[23] In God's grace, a new kingdom culture was created in this community, a culture that is rarely experienced in today's competitive church world. As these gifted young pastors acknowledged their own brokenness before God and before one another, God's healing grace visited us powerfully. The first cohort group completed the Scrubs program in the fall of 2008,[24] but that group continues to meet annually because they have now become a family.

Can we envision having such a pastoral formation experience in many ANA Christian communities? This important task calls for a sustained, collaborative partnership among ANA churches and seminaries working collaboratively to shape and nurture younger pastors and seminarians. In doing so, some of the important themes discussed in this chapter would be very helpful in informing both the process and end goal of such processes. The Scrubs mentoring program, we hope, will be one among many creative pastoral formation programs that would emerge to help ANA churches to nurture and strengthen young pastors.

Conclusion

If ANA churches are to grow as healthy households of God, the task of raising and sustaining healthy pastors is key. While the latest theories in leadership, education, and organizational science might be helpful in sharpening our understanding of pastoral ministry skills, the church's view on the identity of pastor must emerge from the church's sustained reflections on God's Word. For, if church is ultimately not a sociological entity (e.g., "spiritual marketplace") but is theological (e.g., "the household of God"), then the identity of the pastor must ultimately be defined theologically, not sociologically. This chapter, guided by rich insights that emerged from the Pastoral Formation track in the 2009 ANA Consultation of Theology and Ministry, argues that pastors are not hired hands but fellow members of the family, not polished marketing directors but wounded healers. What emerges is a more organic picture of pastors, a picture that highlights God's transformative grace and healing, God's *shalom*.

✦

NOTES

1. This is a fictitious narrative from an ANA church setting.

2. Leader Renewal Institute, Holland, MI, "The Need," www.leaderrenewal.org.

3. *A Summer Health Monitor Report*, Evangelical Lutheran Church of America, 2002.

4. See G. Wagstrom Hallas, *The Right Road—Life Choices for Clergy* (Minneapolis: Augsburg Fortress, 2004), 2–3.

5. William Grosch and David Olsen, "Clergy Burnout: An Integrative Approach," *Journal of Clinical Psychology* 56, no. 5 (2009): 619–32.

6. T. Tseng et al., *Pulpit & Pew: Asian American Religious Leadership Today* (Durham: Duke Divinity School, 2005), 24.

7. According to the *Fact Book on Theological Education*, published by the Association of Theological Schools, there were 577 Asian North American seminarians in the United States and Canada in 1979, 2,065 in 1989, 4,932 in 1999 and 5,203 in 2009. The number peaked in 2003; there were 5,499 ANA seminarians that year.

8. Connie Kang, "Asian American Churches Face Leadership Gap," *Los Angeles Times*, March 3, 2007.

9. Laura Uba, *Asian Americans: Personality Patterns, Identity, and Mental Health* (New York: Guilford, 1994), 28–31.

10. Gordon Fee, *Philippians*, IVP New Testament Commentary Series (Downers Grove, IL: InterVarsity, 1999), 11–37; Frank Thielman, *Philippians*, NIV Application Commentary (Grand Rapids: Zondervan, 1995), 15–29.

11. David Hansen, *The Art of Pastoring: Ministry without All the Answers* (Downers Grove, IL: InterVarsity, 1994), 10.

12. Henri M. Nouwen, *The Wounded Healer: In Our Own Woundedness, We Can Become a Source of Life for Others* (New York: Image, 1979).

13. Yong Kyu Park, *The Great Revivalism in Korea: Its History, Character and Impact, 1901–10* (in Korean; Seoul: Lifebook, 2000), 207–40. To learn about the growing animosity between missionaries and the Korean nationals that peaked before this revival gathering, see Mark Shaw, *Global Awakening: How 20th-Century Revivals Triggered a Christian Revolution* (Downers Grove, IL: InterVarsity, 2010), 38–40.

14. M. Scott Peck, *The Different Drum: Community Making and Peace* (New York: Simon & Schuster, 1987), 86–106.

15. Craig Van Gelder, *The Essence of the Church: A Community Created by the Spirit* (Grand Rapids: Baker, 2000), 23–26.

16. Ibid., 65–69. Peter Berger, a noted sociologist who contributed significantly to the study of religion in modernity, also made a similar observation and identified several key forces of modernity, including the pluralization of religious communities, as the main contributing factor. See Peter Berger, *The Sacred Canopy: Elements of a Sociological Theory of Religion* (New York: Anchor, 1967), 105–53.

17. James B. Twitchell, *Branded Nation: The Marketing of Megachurch, College Inc., and Museum World* (New York: Simon & Schuster, 2004).

18. Ibid., 47–108; Bruce Shelley and Marshall Shelley, *Consumer Church: Can Evangelicals Win the World without Losing Their Souls?* (Downers Grove, IL: InterVarsity, 1992).

19. Van Gelder makes a similar assertion in *Essence of the Church*, 23–26.

20. This exercise, in a slightly different form, appears in Peter Cha, "Student Learning and Formation: An Improvisation Model," in *Revitalizing Practice: Collaborative Models for Theological Faculty*, ed. Malcolm Warford (New York: Peter Lang, 2008), 57, 62–63.

21. Formed in 1991, the Catalyst Leadership Center has aimed to serve the Asian North American Christian community by focusing on the task of mentoring, resourcing, and supporting its leaders.

22. The first cohort group of younger Asian American pastors who participated in this mentoring program came up with the name Scrubs. They explained, "*Scrubs* is our title of choice because it is an honest confession. We are not the gleaming, polished leaders featured in so many leadership conferences. We are 'scrubs': leaders in process; leaders who struggle; leaders who are broken. But rather than seeing this as a liability, we embrace our brokenness as a way of life. We are but 'jars of clay.' And we believe God desires to do an amazing work of grace in us, and through us, that we might touch a deeply broken world."

23. The first module focused on the personal brokenness of the participants while the second module examined the brokenness of our congregations, and the third, the brokenness of our world.

24. In fall 2009 the Catalyst Leadership Center started the second Scrubs mentoring program in the Midwest region. Catalyst is also exploring the possibility of offering a similar mentoring program for ANA women pastors.

CHAPTER 6

✝

The Way Home

Brothers and Sisters Serving Together

GRACE Y. MAY AND PETER K. YI

The way home can be full of anticipation of savory foods, conversations that last late into the night, and being around people who know you well. But the way home can also be long and winding. There are the fears of questions that probe too deeply, the reluctance to engage with certain relations, and the feelings left over from the last gathering. Harmony in the church, like harmony in the family, can be elusive and demand attention that few are eager to give. And yet sacrifice is required for sisters and brothers to sit down at the table together. After all, who wants to give up his seat for a sister when that might mean being relegated to the living room and missing out? Yet often all that is needed is for a brother to pull up an additional chair. Unfortunately, what seems relatively simple to remedy at a dinner table can seem impossible, or even painful, to address in our households of faith.

The difficulty of sisters entering into ministry in Asian churches in North America has been compounded by the divide between egalitarians and complementarians. Egalitarians hold that the Scriptures affirm the equality and full participation of men and women in the church, based on their calling and gifts, not their gender. Complementarians share in the conviction that all people are made in God's image but teach that certain roles in the church are gender specific. What keeps this theological debate from remaining in seminary class rooms and causes it to spill over into the church is the knowledge that decisions reached on women's leadership in the church directly impact over half the people in church, the parameters of one's service, and even the reach of the gospel.

Peter's Journey

My journey with the subject of women in ministry began nearly twenty years ago in an evangelical seminary where the issue was a hot topic of discussion. The professors seemed to be divided on the issue, and as I contemplated the issue for myself, I drew my conclusions based on the influence of my professors and the readings they assigned, my personal upbringing, my personal interaction with relevant biblical texts, and the discussions I had with my seminary peers. My position upon graduating from seminary was that of a staunch complementarian—a position that I carried into my first full-time pastorate.

In my mind, the issue was settled. However, about ten years after my graduation from seminary and well into my ministry, the issue of the ordination of women was brought to the floor of our annual denominational meeting. At that time, I had to ask myself some serious questions. If this issue were to pass, what would I do? Would I remain in the denomination as a silent (or not-so-silent) objector? Or would I take more drastic action and leave the denomination and the church that I had grown to love?

I decided, with a moderate amount of effort, to reopen the files and look at this issue with fresh eyes. As I began my investigation, it dawned on me that I had been quite closed-minded in a prideful way toward people who espoused the egalitarian position. While I had read hundreds of pages on the complementarian position, I had not read a single page on the egalitarian position. So I began to do some reading on the egalitarian position and engage in meaningful discussion with peers who held the egalitarian view. I had to ask myself whether this issue was to me a major or minor doctrinal matter. Was this a theological issue that had immediate gospel ramifications, or was this an issue like paedobaptism where I could agree to disagree? If this was a minor doctrinal issue, and if after my investigation I still remained a complementarian, I was convinced that I could still remain in the denomination with a clear conscience. It took a few more years, but eventually the denominational decision to ordain women for ministry was passed, and our church ordained the first female pastor in our presbytery. Case closed. The issue was once again settled in my mind, or at least I thought it was.

Fast forward to early 2009 when I was asked to be a coauthor for this chapter. At that point in my journey, I was somewhere between a closet complementarian and an unsettled, somewhere-in-between hybrid position. Why, I wondered, would the editors ask *me* to cowrite the chapter on women in ministry? Surely I was more qualified to write on *any* of the other topics.

I now believe this was the providence of God granting me yet another opportunity to look into this important subject. I am convinced it won't be the last time. Working on this writing project has expanded my understanding of the complexities of this issue as never before. Listening to the stories of both men and women (but particularly the women) opened my eyes to the struggles my sisters have experienced in their churches and parachurch organizations alike.

Shortly after our deep and provocative time of sharing, I returned to my church and immediately scheduled a face-to-face meeting with two of my key female leaders and had one email correspondence with a female leader who was away on missions. In these interactions, I asked two questions: (1) Do you feel supported by our church to grow and exercise your giftings and leadership as a woman? (2) Do you feel supported by me, as your lead pastor, to do the same? I had never before asked these questions; it had never dawned on me that they even needed to be asked. I am convinced that I never would have asked these questions if I was not a part of this writing project, for which I am truly grateful.

So regardless of which theological position I have held at any given time, I now believe I can do still more to equip and empower my sisters in fulfilling their callings in the church. That is the journey I am presently on, and the cowriting of this chapter is helping me do that.

We (Peter and Grace) believe that the Scriptures speak to the issues at hand and provide powerful support for greater collaboration and understanding between men and women. The objective here is not necessarily conversion from a complementarian position to the egalitarian view, or vice versa. Regardless of views on gender roles, we seek to present a biblical theology of women's participation in salvation history. What's more, contrary to past and current trends, we strive not to demonize the "other" position, but to subordinate the entire discussion on gender roles under the call to unity in Christ as found in Ephesians 4:1–6:9. The promotion of either position of women's role in the church cannot neglect the prevailing and fundamental call to unity in Christ.

Pointing the Way Home: A Theology of Interdependence

In the household of God, we are brothers and sisters. Our relationship is not based on common kinship or natural bloodlines, but on our identity in Christ. We who were once orphans, through Christ's obedience and death on the cross, are now children (sons *and* daughters) of God (John 1:12). Adopted into God's family, we can now enjoy the privileges and responsibilities of being related to God. Since the beginning, God has demonstrated enormous trust in our forebearers: "God blessed them, and God said to them, '*Be fruitful* and multiply, and fill the earth and subdue it; and *have dominion* over the fish of the sea and over the birds of the air and over every living thing that moves upon the earth'" (Gen. 1:28, NRSV, emphasis ours).

God, then and now, helps us to measure our faithfulness along the twin-axes of *relationship and responsibility*. For example, when we have hurt someone, the degree of willingness and alacrity on our part to apologize or remedy the problem will reflect either poorly or well on our ability to mirror God's forgiveness in our relationships. Or the way we close a deal will reflect how well or poorly we understand God's integrity in carrying out responsibilities entrusted to us. To put it another way, people will see God in us to the extent to which our relationships and responsibilities flow from God's love and rule.

What we discover from the creation narrative is that our gender is actually intrinsic to our identity as image-bearers of God. According to Genesis 1:27: "God created humanity—in his image, in the image of God he created him; male and female he created them" (translation ours).

It is together that we reflect the image of God, not either/or, but "male and female." In our interdependence we reflect the harmony of our triune God; just as the Father, Son, and Spirit relate to one another in perfect love and unity, so should we. Distinct yet one, we are made for one another in marriage, in friendship, and in community. The truth is that our partnership—both in terms of our need and support for one another—reveals in microcosm the community shared by our three-in-one God.

The Prominence of Women Leaders in the Bible

It can be argued that every new era in biblical history begins with a woman. Early on, for example, the Genesis writer alluded to the Messiah coming from Eve's "seed" (Gen. 3:15, KJV; literal meaning of Hebrew). The seed of redemption was promised through Sarah (Gen. 18:10, 14). In Exodus, God raised up no fewer than six women to liberate the Hebrews from slavery: Moses' mother and Miriam strategized to save Moses' life; two midwives, Shiphrah and Puah, defied Pharaoh's edict to kill all Hebrew newborn male infants; and Pharaoh's own daughter, with the aid of her maidservant, rescued the infant Moses and raised him as her own. In Joshua 2, Rahab, the heroine of faith who harbored spies and brought destruction to her own people, ushered in the conquest of the Promised Land. The period of the judges began with Deborah, who was the first judge to be described at length for her spiritual acumen, military prowess, and reign of peace (Judg. 4–5). The Israelite monarchy also began with a woman when God answered Hannah's cry for a child. She gave birth to Samuel, a mighty judge, priest, and prophet, who anointed the first two kings of Israel (1 Sam. 1–2). While in exile, Queen Esther was used providentially to save the Jews from mass destruction, thus enabling the survival of God's people through the postexilic period (Esth. 1-10).

Turning to the New Testament, the Gospel of Luke typifies the prominence of women in the history of salvation by opening with three women—Mary, who gave birth to Jesus; Elizabeth, who gave birth to John the Baptist, and Anna, who verified through prophecy that Jesus was the Messiah (Luke 1:26-28; 1:24-25; 2:36-38). The development of the early church also involved many women, including Nympha, in whose house a fellowship began (Col. 4:15).[1] The very fact that Paul limited the purview of women in the church at Corinth and Ephesus attests to the incredible freedom that women were experiencing in worship and service, and for many, for the very first time. Furthermore, during the early church, persecution did not discriminate between men and women (Acts 8:3), suggesting that the authorities saw both women and men as guilty of spreading the gospel.

But were these women acting as leaders? If by "leadership" we mean in part standing firm in the things of God and influencing the course of history, then the answer is "Yes!" The Old and New Testaments are replete with examples of women leaders—a fact that is all the more astounding given how patriarchal those periods were.

Women in Jesus' Ministry

As we look at Jesus' own ministry, we see how he valued the contributions of both men and women. As the sick and infirm were brought to him, he did not hesitate to heal a hemorrhaging woman or raise a twelve-year-old girl from the dead (Luke 8:40-56). While it would have been outlandish in his day to travel in mixed company in his itinerant ministry, he, nevertheless, sought appropriate venues to teach and interact with women. He met with a Samaritan woman in public in the heat of the noonday sun (John 4:1-26), and he allowed Mary to take the posture of a rabbinical student, sitting at his feet (Luke 10:39, cf. Acts 22:3).[2] Then in contrast to the time-held tradition of only accepting the testimony of men in a court of law, God sovereignly chose women to bear witness to his resurrection (John 20:17-18; Matt. 28:1-10), an honor that signaled Christ's triumph over all the walls that separate humanity from God and from one another.

If we consider Jesus' view of discipleship, "the first shall be last" (Matt. 19:30) and the one who "wants to save his life will lose it, but the one who loses his life will find it" (Matt. 16:25), then what are the implications for women and men in ministry? Jesus repeatedly reminded his disciples to stop jockeying for power, to relinquish control and to become like children. For in God's kingdom, the poor are blessed and the humble raised up; the proud are brought low and the powerful abased. At the conclusion of Matthew's Gospel, Jesus declared, "All authority in heaven and on earth has been given to me; go therefore and make disciples of all nations" (Matt. 28:19). The assumption is that all the power that is needed to evangelize the world resides in Jesus *and* that he will gladly distribute it to his disciples, which he does at Pentecost. Is not the cardinal rule of community to give away what is ours to fill the need in others, so that no one is in want? And isn't the essence of discipleship to empower others to become disciples and full participants of the kingdom?

Distributing and sharing power, however, is costly. Jesus admonishes his disciples to follow in his footsteps: "Greater love has no one than this, to lay down one's life for one's friends" (John 15:13). However, most of us live with a scarcity mentality, which believes that the more you have, the less I will have. But what if we were to choose to live in the light of our God who is infinite in power and wealth, who gives to whom he wants as much as he wants? Then we, as men and women in ministry, would be free to give away power like Jesus and conceive of giving up our own agenda or our seat at the table for another, and thus establish interdependence in our lives and ministries.

Women in Paul's Ministry

Paul stands as a champion for women[3] and wrote the first Christian *magna carta* on equality: "There is no longer Jew or Greek, there is no longer slave or free, there is no longer male and female; for all of you are one in Christ Jesus" (Gal. 3:28). As citizens of the kingdom we are one, whatever our ethnicity, social status, or gender. Paul did not eradicate our differences but simply stated that in our baptism we can lay claim to none of these, for our identity and position in Christ are secured not by any means of our own but wholly by the grace of God. "For by grace are you saved by faith" is the household principle delineated in Ephesians 2:8-9.

What is true of our identity in Christ should, in turn, inform our behavior in the church. We are not locked into responding from a certain social station in life, but are learning to regard ourselves and other members of the household primarily as members of Christ's body. We are encouraged to give honor to the weaker vessel (1 Pet. 3:7) and to seek to correct inequities whether they are found at home or in the larger society.

Paul practiced what he preached. He commenced his missionary work in Europe, in Philippi, where he met Lydia and a group gathered to pray by a riverbank, and then baptized her household (Acts 16:14-15). And he treated women with the same dignity that he treated men, calling Euodia and Syntyche those who "have struggled beside me in the work of the gospel" (Phil. 4:3), and at the same time, not shying away from urging them as leaders in the church to be united (Phil. 4:2). He acknowledged Priscilla as well as her husband Aquila as teachers (Acts 18:26).[4] He greeted female and male coworkers by name, and even topped his list of colleagues in Romans 16 with Phoebe, a minister of the church in Cenchrea (Rom. 16:1), and he mentioned Junia, a female apostle (Rom 16:7). Paul's practice was to publicly recognize his sisters in ministry.

Overcoming Roadblocks

Over and against the evidence from our bird's eye view of the biblical and theological evidence for women in leadership, it became apparent from the stories in our focus group at the consultation that a dearth of women leaders in ANA churches remains. Roadblocks still confront men and women who want to see women lead in the church. While there are many contributing factors, we will focus on three: (1) our cultural assumptions about gender and leadership, (2) our initiative in calling and empowering women to lead, and (3) our family responsibilities and expectations.

Our Cultural Assumptions about Gender and Leadership

Jesus boldly and unapologetically challenged the leadership paradigms of his day and he did not impose gender-specific expectations upon leaders. Instead he taught universal principles of leadership. To be great, you must be a servant. The Son of Man came not to be served but to serve. And he poignantly demonstrated servant-leadership when he got down on his knees and washed his disciples' feet (John 13:3-5).

Yet many of us have bought into our ANA culture's assumptions about gender and leadership. For example, we accept a loud voice or aggressive behavior as authoritative when it comes from a man, but not from a woman. We expect a woman to defer to her male colleagues and sometimes even to her male subordinates, but not the other way around. Or women may tend to accept leadership positions that are more "behind the scenes" when they might actually be more gifted in more visible leadership roles.

As Nikki Toyama-Szeto, Urbana Program Director for InterVarsity Christian Fellowship, astutely observed, general cultural expectations put women at a disadvantage in becoming leaders within the church, because "in North American culture Asian women are stereotyped to be kind and docile." The perception in ANA culture is that "leadership should be reserved for men," so consequently "when women become assertive and take initiative, they suddenly become masculine."[5] When this perception is then imported into the church and overlaid with the Christian virtue of humility, everyone expects women to be demure, conciliatory, and soft-spoken—

anything but assertive. ANA women, consciously or not, internalize this culturally-defined posture.

Women and Men Taking Initiative

Almost across the board in ANA (and other) churches, men are the gatekeepers. The problem is that they have often left the doors of leadership closed to women. Because they do not feel the frustration of being excluded, many male leaders have not seen the need to provide a venue for women to voice their concerns and opinions, much less to lead. In many churches, women might not even be invited to the conversation, which nixes any desire on the part of women to even give any kind of input.

When women *are* elected or appointed to places of leadership, they are often not accorded the same prerogative as their male colleagues to set the agenda. Kevin Doi, a pastor and a participant in the ANA consultation, raised some incisive questions: "I keep thinking about issues of power. Who ends up making decisions on behalf of others? Who gets to be in the conversation? The other thing I realized is, who gets to ask the question about what we talk about? Maybe another way to swing it is, who is allowed to make mistakes? This is [about] power, too, but it is also [about] permission and space."[6]

The right to make decisions and to make mistakes add up to who has the de facto power in the board room or pastoral staff meeting. Where are the "Pauls" of our church who will create the space for women, not only to enter the dialogue but also to shape the content and direction of the discussion? The point here is that very little will change unless men take the initiative of paving the way. For example, the church needs men who will elect and recommend female leaders for leadership positions. It needs godly men in leadership to encourage women to pursue God's call on their lives.

Once leadership creates the space, the challenge is for women to step into that space. As Justine Han, a veteran campus staff minister, asserts, "Women need to courageously offer themselves as equal partners in ministry even if no one offers them the opportunity. If women passively wait for that opportunity to come their way, it may never arrive. The women of the church need to go ahead and offer their gifts and their leadership."[7]

Where are the "Eunices" and "Loises" in the church—older sisters who identify younger sisters and brothers and pour into their lives? The cry for mentors continues to go up. We need women who will answer by nurturing, teaching, and shepherding others. Women can disciple over a cup of coffee or in an accountability group. And churches and pastors can foster a culture of discipleship by blessing both informal and structured forms of discipleship.

Expectations at Different Seasons

As members of the same household, brothers and sisters need to appreciate the expectations and special burdens that certain seasons of life bring. As supportive as a husband may want to be, he may still struggle with his wife's giftedness. For example, consider a couple in which the husband is the classic engineer type and the wife has leadership gifts. When she is nominated to be a deacon, she declines. In fact, she actually downplays her leadership abilities to avoid overshadowing her husband. In turn, he fears that her authority to make decisions at church would detract from their marriage. Or in another scenario, a woman is asked to take charge of a large conference. While her husband is not comfortable with this arrangement, he proposes that the following year they lead together. Then there are families that cannot afford to have both parents serving at church at the same time without impairing their family life, and it is usually the women who end up meeting the needs of the home.

Our hope would be that after much prayer, both the husband and wife would be able to find a mutually acceptable solution. Serving together as a family is much more of a dance than a science. A dance is filled with variations at different life stages. As families go through life stages—get married, have their first child, change careers, care for their own parents, fall sick, or retire—the availability for service in the church changes for husbands and wives.

The rhythm, of course, will also vary with each family. We have both advised engaged couples about the importance of dividing household duties according to giftedness and preference. For example, a wife with a background in finances might balance the checkbook, while a husband who starts work later in the day might take care of the children's lunches. Then other daily tasks, such as preparing meals, doing the laundry, taking out the garbage, and driving the children to afterschool activities might be shared between the two.

Different challenges face singles in the church. Do they have a place in the church to exercise their gifts; more specifically, do singles whose gifts lie in leadership have a place to exercise their gifts? Do the younger sisters have mentors from whom they can grow and learn? Moreover, do churches know how to minister to and minister with single women (never married or otherwise) in their forties or fifties? The answers to such questions can make all the difference in the world to a sister struggling to see her place in the household of God.

Bridging the Gap between our Explicit and Implicit Theology

In light of the cultural blind spots of the ANA church regarding the issue of women in leadership, there exists a disjuncture between the biblical evidence and our practice. In other words, our explicit and implicit theologies are not always in harmony. Implicit theology—what our actions reveal about what we really believe—speaks louder and is more influential than our explicit theology—what our official statements say we believe.

For example, in a recent Advent service, all of the candlelighters were boys. While the church in no way intended to say that only boys were fit to be candlelighters, the implicit message was that the church favored the participation of boys. Another example is when a church affirms women in ministry but rarely ever preaches or teaches about women in the Bible or lifts up examples of faith who are women. The church is not deliberately omitting women in biblical history or as positive role models, but the implicit message is that they are not as important as the men.

Advocating for consistency in both our explicit and implicit theology, Lisa Sung, who teaches theology at Trinity Evangelical Divinity School, explained:

> The absence of an explicit theology on this matter will basically lead to a lack of accountability among the leaders of the church. They can continue living in the gray, avoiding the issue, and as a result, confuse both the men and women of the church. Instead, the leaders of the church need to boldly state the church's position on this important issue. Then the whole congregation can move toward living out an implicit theology in the life of the church. Without an explicit theology on the subject of women in the church, we will continue to perpetuate doing things in the ways they have always been done.[8]

Bridging our implicit and explicit theologies can be done. For example, I (Grace) was called several years ago to be a pastor at my home church, a congregation that has never ordained women and where women do not administer communion or baptism. The implicit message is ambiguous: do we or do we not affirm women in ministry? The compromise solution seems to be that the church accepts female pastors, but they do not have all the privileges of their male colleagues. So after preaching and shepherding for over a year, I decided to offer a series on "Paul, Gender, and Relationships." The goal was to make explicit a theology that supports women in ministry from the Scriptures.

After having met with the female leaders in our church, I (Peter) concluded that the church leadership really hadn't made clear what position it had taken on women in ministry. There was a lack of articulation, which came off as ambiguity. We engage in certain practices, but our theology has not caught up with them yet. For instance, we see women leading women's ministry, but we do not see enough of them leading ministries for the whole congregation. As the senior pastor, I plan on changing this approach in order to bridge the gap between what we practice and what we say we believe.

Homeward Bound

What was probably most rewarding in our forum was hearing one another's stories and being able to appreciate the positive and the negative aspects of our respective journeys into ministry and wholeness. To be heard was a gift. To have men ask women to help them understand was a unique experience for some. Creating a respectful space where honest conversation could happen allowed us to speak to the real issues and even confront the pain that is so often dismissed or ignored. Author James Baldwin wrote, "Not everything that is faced can be changed. But nothing can be changed unless it is faced."[9] Building on this quotation, Lisa Sung led us into an eloquent summary of our forum discussion:

> As Asian Americans, we don't like to rock the boat. We hold back from naming the brokenness, out of politeness and reluctance to criticize. But unless and until we face and name the implicit practices that keep women in bondage, those who groan inwardly from being stymied will continue to suffer in silence rather than receiving healing and blessing in Christ. And collectively, without harnessing all that these godly, gifted women have to contribute, the church will keep attempting to minister with one hand tied behind its back—limping along, when we could be personifying as well as proclaiming the gospel that reconciles men and women with God and with one another, in Christ.[10]

Our willingness to confront our frustration and pain, rather than maintaining a veneer of respect, will allow men and women to go beyond the surface and explore more deeply who we are and who we can be. In the forum, we did not just focus on the problems, but we also dreamed of a better future. The first step toward that hope was hearing one another's stories. When we listen to the voices of sisters and brothers, then we show that the church values all God's children. When we create a safe space for people to exercise their gifts and mature in their faith, then we become more fully the people whom God wants us to be. Finally, when sisters and brothers can feel at home exercising their gifts and growing together, as members of Christ's body, we can present to the world a most compelling presentation of the gospel.

Imagine a church where women and men could be encouraged to explore the issues around gender together and with a desire to learn and grow in the process. Imagine a church that would be so committed to God's vision for relationships and responsibilities that they would be open to changing their attitudes and behavior toward men and women. Imagine a church that would actually be a pacesetter in the area of gender, where others would flock precisely because they have heard that the way they treat one another is different from the world.

The place to begin for many ANA churches is at the level of leadership. Our spiritual fathers as well as spiritual mothers need to teach and promote fuller participation of women in ministry. As leaders we need to demonstrate that we value both men and women serving in the church by giving others opportunities to minister. Whether we are egalitarian or complementarian, we can all strive for greater inclusion of women in our ministries. To do this, our leaders will also need the courage to clarify their own positions, not fearing disagreement from the congregation and not being afraid of costly changes.

The household of God presents a powerful example of inclusion and an alternative community to our biological or nuclear family, where fathers and/or mothers may have been absent physically, emotionally, or spiritually, or worse, abusive. Jesus said, pointing to his disciples, "Whoever does the will of my Father in heaven is my brother and sister and mother" (Matt. 12:48-50, NRSV). In Jesus' family, there all kinds of people, but they are united by the common vision of the kingdom where members are willing to divest themselves of power in order to give power to those with less power. Those called to lead God's household are *door openers* who are willing to affirm and equip up-and-coming leaders, male and female; they are *pastor-shepherds* who encourage sisters as well as brothers to utilize their gifts to the fullest; they are *mentors* who train brothers to respect sisters and make room for them at the table where decisions are made; they are *advocates* who agitate for change on behalf of marginalized women; they are *reconcilers* who are adept at brokering the power of the cross; and they are *pioneers* who are not afraid of being the first to model gender reconciliation in their communities. It is our hope that ANA churches would be full of such men and women.

Grace's Journey

When I was four years old, while other children were playing house, I arranged small chairs in a row, took my place in front of them, and started preaching at them. When I was seven, my Sunday school teacher's wife asked me what I wanted to be when I grew up; when I replied that I wanted to be a pastor, she responded, "Girls don't do that." I didn't object or ask why, but that's when I started dreaming of becoming other things, like an astronaut and later a psychologist. But the one constant in my journey—from VBS to youth group through my college days—was the joy I found in serving Christ and seeing people grow in their love for God. In trying to discern my call, I sought the counsel of many people whom God had brought into my life, and finally two years after graduation I started seminary, buoyed by the prayers and support of my home church.

I enrolled in seminary with the desire to be equipped so that I could return and serve our church in ministry. Little did I know how circuitous the road would be. At seminary I delved into the original languages to understand Paul's teaching on women in the church and discovered just how challenging the passages were exegetically. But I grossly underestimated how intricate and enmeshed the subject of men and women in the church was. There were so many variables that influence how men and women perceive the opposite gender: family background, relationships with parents, male and female role models, positive and negative experiences with both genders, cultural expectations of men and women, gender stereotyping, and not least of all, the perspective of church leaders, ecclesial tradition, and denominational affiliation. Thankfully, I met fellow pilgrims, godly mentors, teachers, and pastors, both men and women, who based their views not on society's norms but on their biblical convictions.

Even after poring over the Scriptures and coming to the conclusion that God did call women to be pastors, I had *one* further question: Was God calling *me*? The answer was fraught with difficulties, because I was prone to second-guess myself, to assume my aspirations were motivated by pride, and to wonder if I could ever complete the journey. After all, when I graduated in the early 1990s, as far as I knew, no independent, evangelical Chinese church on the East Coast was ordaining women. The ANA church, then and now, has a great need for pastors. Yet it seems, even today, the only criterion that keeps most churches from even considering candidates like me is our gender.

After struggling for two more years, I started doctoral studies, thinking that if I could not pastor, then perhaps, I could at least teach pastors. At the same time that I resumed my studies, God led me to worship and serve at an African American church. What a boon that was to my spirit! Through the embrace of the congregation and the opportunities given to me assisting the pastor, leading congregational prayer, praying with individuals, counseling, preaching, and doing visitations, I came to realize how much I relished pastoral ministry. The mentoring and encouragement I received from both the pastor and the congregation confirmed my sense of calling. God was restoring and even augmenting my joy.

Months before I graduated, God turned the tables on me. To my surprise, an independent, evangelical Chinese church on the East Coast called me. Then, after pastoring at that church for over five years, the Lord graciously opened the door for me to teach at a seminary. And some twenty years after I embarked on my journey into ministry and entered seminary, the Lord led me back to my home church to pastor the English congregation. At every stage of my journey, God provided brothers and sisters as door openers, supporters, advocates, friends, mentors, and pioneers. I am who I am because our God is merciful and gracious and is determined to lavish love on all his children. I see my journey as a personal quest and as part of a larger call to discipleship for all who yearn to be true to Christ.

Returning Home: Taking the Next Steps

Our prayer is that the journey does not have to be so painful or long for others. Indeed, it was heartening to find in our focus group that the road has already gotten easier for those coming after us. Historically parachurch organizations have been more affirming of the gifts of both genders, but our dream is that soon our own churches might become places of acceptance and affirmation for both men and women.

What constitutes part of the cutting edge of the gospel in the twenty-first century? We believe it is sisters and brothers serving *together*, supporting one another, being honest about their brokenness, bringing healing, living in freedom, and fulfilling their calling. Let us drink deeply of the Spirit, who can lead us together in this dance of life that mirrors the life of the Trinity, overflowing with love and truth. May God dwell among us richly so we can truly experience home en route to our eternal home.

For those on a similar journey of discovery with regard to women in leadership, we conclude our chapter not with conclusions but with questions. Hopefully, the following questions will lead to some practical and concrete steps in becoming a healthier household of God where sisters and brothers love and serve one another.

1. If you are a leader, how can you teach about the subject of women in leadership with greater clarity? What kinds of resources would broaden or deepen your convictions on the matter? How can you begin developing an explicit theology of women in leadership at your church and then begin teaching on it?

2. If you are a male leader, how could you champion the cause of women in your sphere of influence? What does it cost brothers to make a decision? What kind of work and intentionality is required? How could you identify the gifts of prospective female leaders?

3. If you are a female leader, how could you take more initiative in your own growth? How can you set an example for other women and make a difference for those who come after you?

4. Whether you are a male or female leader, what are ways you can proactively show greater respect for female leaders? Is there any area in which the Holy Spirit is calling you to repentance?

5. If you are a seminarian, what courses would better inform your theology of women in ministry?

6. Historically, as churches became more institutionalized, women became increasingly marginalized in the leadership structure. How might that knowledge impact changes that you attempt in your church, business, school, or other institutional setting?

7. Practically, how have groups you belong to extended the invitation to lead to women or grown in their inclusion of women in leadership? What kinds of responsibilities are women entrusted with? How could you make greater progress in developing a culture that affirms sisters and brothers?

8. What kinds of ministries would encourage the spiritual growth of women in different seasons of their lives, for example, single, married, mothers, widowed, or retired?

9. How do you think God is asking you to respond to your church's position on the ordination of women?

10. Calling upon your understanding of racial reconciliation, when might it be appropriate to issue a public apology for sexism? What would that look like in your community?

11. Take opportunities to share about women who have made a difference in your life and have served as trail blazers, godly examples, and encouragers.

✦
NOTES

1. For a more detailed history of the relationship between women and the origins of house churches, see Kevin Giles, "House Churches," *Priscilla Papers* 24 (Winter 2010): 6–8; Carolyn Osiek, Margaret Y. McDonald, and Janet H. Tulloch, *A Woman's Place: House Churches in Earliest Christianity* (Minneapolis: Fortress, 2006).

2. For further historical background on the practice of sitting at a teacher's feet, see Aida B. Spencer, *Beyond the Curse: Women Called to Ministry* (Peabody, MA: Hendrickson, 1985), 57–61.

3. See James R. Beck and Craig L. Blomberg, *Two Views on Women in Ministry* (Grand Rapids: Zondervan, 2001).

4. In four of the six instances that Priscilla and Aquila's names appear in the New Testament, her name appears first, suggesting that she may have been the lead teacher.

5. Nikki Toyama-Szeto, "Women in Ministry Track," Catalyst ANA Consultation, May 2009, Deerfield, IL.

6. Kevin Doi, "Women in Ministry Track," Catalyst ANA Consultation, May 2009, Deerfield, IL.

7. Justine Han, "Women in Ministry Track," Catalyst ANA Consultation, May 2009, Deerfield, IL.

8. Lisa Sung, "Women in Ministry Track," Catalyst ANA Consultation, May 2009, Deerfield, IL.

9. James Baldwin, *The Cross of Redemption*, ed. Randall Kenan (New York: Pantheon, 2010), 34.

10. Sung, "Women in Ministry Track," Catalyst ANA Consultation, May 2009, Deerfield, IL.

CHAPTER 7

✝

Formation of Servants in God's Household

NANCY SUGIKAWA AND
M. SYDNEY PARK

Jessica, a young adult worship leader in a Chinese American church, has a different vision for Sunday worship than her church pastors and elders. Her attempts at making worship more energetic and passionate have resulted in complaints that the drums are too loud, the singing is too long, and there aren't enough hymns on Sunday. Apart from disagreements over worship style, Jessica also feels that she is not included in leadership discussions or significant decisions about the future of the church. Jessica is discouraged and frustrated, complaining frequently about the church's lack of cultural relevance and spiritual depth. She attends an independent small group with a dozen other young adults from various churches. Like several of her friends, Jessica is thinking about finding another church where her worship, spiritual, and social needs will be met, but she feels guilty about leaving the church in which she has grown up.

Steve became a Christian five years ago through a friend who invited him to church. He began serving almost immediately and has now been leading the usher team for more than two years. Steve has two young children but gets to church early on Sunday to help set up every week. He has tried to get other people to help, but no one seems to be as committed as he is. Steve's wife, Susan, is also a young believer. She was supportive of his church commitments in the beginning but has now grown tired of his frequent absences from home. She feels that Steve prioritizes church over their family and is too much of a perfectionist. They argue often, and she recently brought up the issue of divorce. As an Asian American, Steve is too ashamed to talk about his marital problems, so no one in their couple's small group knows about their struggles. In the meantime, Steve feels overwhelmed and confused about what to do.

Like many Asian North American (ANA) lay leaders, Jessica and Steve have not found ministry in the church easy. They began their journey into leadership encouraged to contribute their gifts and abilities to build up the church. But along the way, the weight of leadership has been made heavier by cultural and generational challenges.

Younger leaders like Jessica find themselves struggling for autonomy and empowerment in the midst of a hierarchical ethnic culture that often values age over vision, experience over passion, and tradition over innovation. These leaders find that their quest for a seat at the true leadership table is often frustrated as they are relegated to ministry on the sidelines—children, youth, worship, and missions—without a real voice or power to make significant changes in the direction of the church.

Other leaders like Steve approach ministry the same way they approach their secular work, with a high work ethic combined with the call to serve God wholeheartedly. But the fear of failure and pressure to excel sometimes prove too costly and stressful for leadership to be sustained. Once someone accepts responsibility for a ministry, they are often left to figure things out by themselves. The growth of their inner spiritual life, as well as of their family relations, is often neglected as they focus on the tasks at hand. Their pastors and other lay leaders are usually too busy themselves to nurture, train, or equip them for lasting ministry. And the drive toward perfectionism prohibits transparency concerning personal and family struggles.

How can we change the status quo and breathe new life into the formation of lay leaders in God's household? How do we understand the foundation of saving grace, unity, and self-sacrifice when it comes to equipping the whole body for ministry? We must first address the cultural and theological challenges that distort God's intention for a healthy context of leadership formation. Then we must commit to investing in and developing lay leaders in grace-filled learning environments informed by mutual brokenness, healing, and reconciliation.

ANA Leadership in the Church: An Imperfect Model

Ephesians 2 reminds believers that we are saved by grace, not as a result of our performance or anything we have achieved. We are unconditionally loved, redeemed, chosen, and blessed. We are lovingly adopted into a new family centered on the generosity and kindness of God himself (John 1:12; 1 John 3:1). As members of God's household, we learn new ways of relating to one another and to the world. We are called toward a Christ-centered life marked by a new mission (Acts 1:8), the call to love one another (John 13:34-35; Eph. 4:1-16), make disciples of all nations (Matt. 28:18-20), and care for the least, the last, and the lost, including those whom we have never even met (Matt. 25:34-40).

But embracing a new identity, family, and mission while growing up in the household of God can be challenging, especially for Asians growing up in North America. The pain and brokenness of our personal, family, or ethnic story often hinders us from experiencing the full blessings of Christ-centered community, especially when it comes to ministry and leadership development.

The Struggle for Honor and Respect

As many of our families emigrated from Asia to the West over the last hundred years, immigrant Christian churches began to emerge all over the United States and Canada. In these ANA churches, people gathered in community with fellow immigrants, speaking a common language, eating familiar foods, and identifying with similar challenges of enculturation. Parents maintained hopes that their children would have a better life economically and marry those with a similar ethnic background. They upheld the cultural practices and values of their ethnic roots as their Christian communities became social oases for those seeking sanctuary from the hostilities of an unfamiliar land.[1]

More recently, Asian families who immigrated to the West often came from positions of status and affluence. In their native countries, these adult immigrants might have been doctors, educators, or successful businesspersons. But in their new homeland, immigrant parents usually had to reestablish themselves by opening small businesses, such as dry cleaners or restaurants, that required little formal education or English language skills. The underlying desire to reestablish social status, power, and comfort so often denied to ethnic minorities was (and still is) difficult to surrender.[2]

The immigrant church therefore provided a safe place where a person could find reprieve from feelings of inadequacy, and their intelligence, experience, or giftedness could still be appreciated. In the church, one who was "unseen" in mainstream society could finally be "seen"; one who was undervalued by the world's standards could be esteemed though ministry faithfulness. Those who were powerless in society (immigrants, non-English speakers, and the elderly) could find affirmation and influence among their peers.

Leadership in the church became a form of recognition not only of one's holiness and faithfulness but of one's value in society. Therefore, those who achieved positions of leadership in the church often hid their weaknesses and inadequacies in order to gain or maintain public honor and respect. A cultural fear of shame or public humiliation made it even more difficult for church leaders to find safe places to honestly express fears, admit failures, or confess their need for help.

The result is that many second- and third-generation ANA leaders are hesitant to take risks in life and in ministry. The fear of disclosure and a drive to keep up an illusion of competence and confidence make it difficult to cultivate authenticity and transparency in the church. Emotional, relational, and even spiritual struggles remain hidden and often denied. Even when leaders become aware of their personal brokenness, there are few resources to help them process their past hurts and move toward true healing and wholeness.

However, striving for the illusion of power, respect, and honor, especially that found in leadership positions, stands in opposition to the values of brokenness and interdependence so central to the way of Jesus. Despite their immigrant history, can the ANA church leadership more faithfully reflect the "downward mobility" of the incarnation that embraces brokenness and clings to God's promise in 2 Corinthians 12:9, "My grace is sufficient for you, for my power is made perfect in weakness"? (ESV). How can leaders be encouraged to trust in God's faithfulness to work out his purposes not just despite but through their weaknesses and inadequacies? How can leadership find healing and wholeness even as they are instruments of healing and wholeness in others?

Self-Preservation or Self-Sacrifice

An issue closely related to the struggle for honor and respect is that of self-preservation. Although they no doubt had a desire to reach out to others with the gospel message, for ANA Christian immigrants, the good news of Jesus Christ was directed primarily at family members, friends, and fellow immigrants. Those who rose to leadership in the church were usually members who valued cultural traditions and respected the sacrifices made by the first generation. Leadership was given primarily to those who had earned enough social favor or had just lived longer than everyone else.

Over time, cultural and language differences began to emerge in immigrant families, where first-generation parents became overly dependent on their children who more easily assimilated and learned English. These parents' need for recognition, especially after their immense sacrifices, often went unnoticed and unappreciated in their homes and even in the church. The support of hierarchy and patriarchy in the church sometimes became a cry for respect and appreciation from those who had endured much humiliation and sacrifice.

At the same time, younger leaders in the church often feel that their faithful service and contributions are not enough to earn them a right to be heard. Their needs and desires are overlooked in favor of the status quo. For first-generation immigrants, leadership in the church is often a symbol of social status and the power to preserve immigrant culture and language rather than a recognition of one's call and spiritual gifting to equip the whole body for works of service (Eph. 4:11-16). For younger leaders, leadership in the church is seen as an opportunity to bring needed change and become more culturally relevant for their generation.

These differences in values and the struggle to obtain affirmation and resources result in tensions between developing leaders and gatekeepers within the church. Distrust and competition become roadblocks to honest communication and authentic friendships between generations.

Without an outlet for the fulfillment of their own visions and passions, many second- and third-generation leaders leave their immigrant communities, joining or planting English-speaking ANA and multiethnic congregations. The experience and spiritual maturity of older generations are lost, and these young leaders are often left to develop on their own. Their longing for parental affirmation and blessing in their calling and mission remain unmet.

So often within the ANA church, leadership among first as well as subsequent generations has more to do with self-preservation than it does with self-sacrifice or selfless devotion to Christ and others. Yet Mark 10:42-46 reminds us of what Jesus taught his disciples: "You know that those who are regarded as rulers of the Gentiles lord it over them, and their high officials exercise authority over them. Not so with you. Instead, whoever wants to become great among you must be your servant, and whoever wants to be first must be slave of all. For even the Son of Man did not come to be served, but to serve, and to give his life as a ransom for many" (NIV). In a parallel passage in Luke 22:24-26, Jesus says, "Instead, the greatest among you should be like the *youngest*, and the one who rules like the one who serves" (NIV, emphasis added). In Jewish patriarchal and hierarchical society, these were controversial words indeed!

How must leadership in the church better reflect the model of self-sacrifice in Ephesians 5:1-2 that Jesus demonstrated on behalf of those he loved? How do we practice reconciliation and unity that seeks to understand rather than be understood, to honor rather than seek honor, to give rather than receive? How can those in power use their influence not to maintain control but to provide safe places for younger leaders to experiment and meet the needs of their own generation?

Embracing the Biblical Call to Humility and Selfless Service

To address the two issues raised above, we will focus on Paul's letter to the Philippians. Paul has an interesting story to tell us in Philippians 3:2-11. This is a rare instance where Paul shares his own biographical sketch of how his life changed as a result of his conversion.[3] It is a good example of how one's personal and national identity changes as a result of knowing Christ. We begin with a brief description of Philippians 2.

In his letter to the Philippians, Paul provides positive examples of faithfulness for the Philippians to adopt (2:6-11,19-30; 3:3-11). The primary example is that of Christ in Philippians 2:6-8. Although Jesus Christ has equality with God (v. 6), he does not use this privilege as an occasion for self-promotion or self-glory.[4] Rather, he sees his equality with God as the foundation for extraordinary humility (vv. 7-8). Christ not only takes the form of a slave,[5] but takes on the likeness of humanity (incarnation) and humbles himself even further by becoming obedient even to the point of death. This is the model Paul exhorts the Philippians to adopt for healthy, indeed proper communal relations within the community of God (2:1-5).[6] And as we look to 2:9-11, we see that this extreme humility is the disposition that God honors: "Therefore God has highly exalted him and bestowed on him the name that is above every name" (ESV).

In Philippians 2:19-30, Paul provides two other positive examples patterned after the model of Christ: Timothy and Epaphroditus.[7] Both men demonstrate the selflessness of Christ and serve those within the community of God even at the risk of losing their own lives (vv. 27,30). For both men, the primary concern is not to seek their own interest, glory, and honor, but those of Christ's (vv. 20-21).

From these three examples we see that the claim that we are saved by Jesus Christ necessarily means that we no longer seek selfish interests: self-glory, self-honor, and even self-preservation. Christ obeys to the point of death, even death on the cross (2:8). Timothy serves not his own interest but the interests of others and serves God and Paul as a slave would serve his master (2:21-22).[8] Epaphroditus is willing to risk his own life for the work of Christ and fellow believers (2:29-30). And these examples of life sacrificed stand in coherence with Jesus' words: "Whoever wants to be my disciple must deny themselves and take up their cross and follow me. For whoever wants to save their life will lose it, but whoever loses their life for me and for the gospel will save it" (Mark 8:34-36, NIV). To be saved is to deny oneself and follow in the pattern of Christ.

Does the call to sacrifice extend even to the cultural issues of honor and shame or the concern to preserve family and ethnic tradition? Paul's testimony in Philippians 3:2-11 provides some insight to this question. Paul has already provided three positive examples. But in Philippians 3:2, he turns to a negative example (those who advocate circumcision) before offering his own life as a model in verses 4-11. In the harsh words of 3:3, Paul warns that those who advocate the necessity of circumcision are mistakenly putting confidence in the flesh. Now at this point, for the modern-day reader, the concept of "confidence in the flesh" might be a bit vague; what precisely does Paul mean by these words? Paul sets it in opposition to "worship by the Spirit of God" and "boast/glory in Christ Jesus." So, the phrase "confidence in the flesh" is set in contrast to "boast/glory in Christ Jesus" (3:3).[9] This contrast is further explained in verses 4-11.

Paul states in 3:3-4 that while he does not place confidence in the flesh, he has every reason to do so. Certainly, his confidence is even greater than most can boast, and in 3:5-6 he provides the basis for this confidence: (1) circumcised on the eighth day; (2) member of the people of Israel; (3) from the tribe of Benjamin; (4) a Hebrew of Hebrews; (5) as to the law, a Pharisee; (6) as to zeal, a persecutor of the church; and (7) as to righteousness, under the law blameless.

All these attributes are based on Paul's cultural identity as a member of the chosen race, Israel, the people of God. But Paul's honor is not simply based on the general cultural identity of being an Israelite. In the fourth and fifth attributes, he states that he comes from the elite class even among the Israelites. As a Pharisee, he would have had a keen interest in purity and holiness of God by keeping the law even down to the minutiae. From this point, he moved on toward attributes particular to himself. His passionate cultural allegiance led to persecuting the church (cf. Acts 8:1-3; 9:1-2). And in the last attribute, he makes a bold statement that very few Hebrews could claim, "as to righteousness, under the law blameless." Both of these attributes, according to the Hebrew culture, are virtues on which honor is based. But what happens to these cultural virtues, these points of personal honor when Paul encounters Christ?

In the following verses, Paul asserts that the advantages he enjoyed are now viewed from a different perspective for the sake of Christ: they are no longer virtues, but "losses" (3:7). In 3:8, Paul goes even further; he uses the word *skubalon*, which receives a sanitized translation of "rubbish" in most translations, but it more accurately refers to "refuse, dung, feces." What makes Paul reconsider what appears to be by all accounts excellent pedigree and admirable achievements as excrement? He lists one primary reason: Jesus Christ. For Paul, all virtues and advantages that we may have in ourselves, whether national or personal, become liabilities in view of the incomparable worth of knowing Christ Jesus (3:8). And "being found in Christ" meant having a righteousness of God that comes from faith in lieu of having a righteousness that comes from law observance (3:9). The process of conversion to Christian faith mandates this exchange of cultural values for the surpassing greatness of knowing Christ.[10] Do we know this Christ? Is the knowledge of this Christ worth relinquishing all our honor, virtue, and merit? For Paul, this transformation of values is part and parcel of salvation.

Spirituality Based on Works Instead of Grace

It is easy to forget that Christians are people under grace and not under law. Because ANA families often have a strong work ethic and value diligence and perseverance, many ANA individuals live under constant pressure to excel and perform. Asian parents often compare the accomplishments of their children with one another, perhaps to gain recognition of their many sacrifices for a better life for their offspring. In fact, receiving good grades in school, obtaining a high-paying job, or producing healthy grandchildren are ways many ANA young adults communicate gratitude to their parents and win their approval. On the other hand, failure to achieve or fulfill parental hopes or expectations can cause individuals to develop a nagging feeling that love is conditional and based on how well they perform.

Even in the church, ANA Christians often struggle with an unconscious drive to succeed and excel in whatever they do. They live with an almost constant sense of guilt or shame, feeling that they ought to be more spiritual, to sin less, and to give more sacrificially toward God's ministry. The burden of duty or obligation in family life and ministry hinders many believers from finding security in loving relationship with God alone. The belief that what one does *for* God is really what qualifies one to be *with* God is difficult to shake. Ministry and even spiritual practices can be reduced to spiritualized work that believers hope will earn them praise, respect, and even love in God's household.

At the same time, whether it is leading a small group or becoming an elder, church members are often afraid to be identified as leaders because deep down they know they are not the person they appear to be. They avoid the light of scrutiny and are fearful of disappointing those they desperately want to please or impress. They do not want to bring shame and dishonor to those they love when hidden sins, addiction, or character flaws are discovered.

Some church members cling to spiritual adolescence, refusing to enter the adult world, which expects too much of them and is less forgiving when they make mistakes. Becoming a spiritual leader is too burdensome and costly. These spiritual teenagers choose instead to stay on the sidelines, voicing criticisms of those in power but afraid to act and risk failure themselves.

Those who do step into leadership often put immense pressure on themselves to perform with excellence and perfection in everything they attempt. Their struggle to appear successful and spiritual often results in unhealthy habits and self-imposed perfectionism that cannot be sustained. Admitting failure or asking for help is often equated with giving up in defeat and imposing the heavy burden of leader-ship on someone else. Even stepping down or taking a break from leadership is not an easy option because of feelings of failure and inadequacy. In the meantime, many leaders neglect the care of their own souls and keep their struggles hidden from those closest to them.

How do we redefine leadership such that it becomes less bur-densome? How do we nurture authenticity, recognizing that we are people of grace and do not need to do anything to earn God's favor? How can we trust the outrageous love and generosity of God that invites us to join him in the redemptive activity he is already accom-plishing in us and through us?

Lessons from Heroes of Faith

In the Christian tradition, names like Abraham, Moses, and David in the Old Testament and Peter, John, and James—the inner circle of the twelve apostles in the New Testament—have become familiar names linked with the notions of "faithfulness" and perhaps "righ-teousness." In the Old Testament, Abraham, Moses, and David all faithfully served God and are known as the pillars of Israel's faith. In the New Testament, Peter, John, and James were the "elite among the elite." These three were privileged among the other Twelve and enjoyed particular favor from Jesus; for example, they alone saw the transfigured Jesus (Mark 9:2-13); they were selected to follow Jesus to Jairus's house (Mark 5:37); and they closely accompanied Jesus to pray in Gethsemane (Mark 14:33). Although James died early (Acts 12:1-2), Peter and John became pillars of the early church (Gal. 2:9). Clearly all these characters are justifiably called "heroes of faith."

Yet, Scripture, Old and New, does not whitewash any of these champions, but portrays them in stark realism. Moses was not only a murderer and a fugitive (Exod. 2:11-15), he had a stubborn streak that provoked God's anger (Exod. 4:1-17). David, in spite of God's great favor, committed adultery with Bathsheba and conspired to murder her husband, Uriah (2 Sam. 11:1-27). In the New Testa-ment, Peter, called the "Rock" by Jesus (Matt. 16:13-19), failed more than he succeeded in understanding Jesus and the life of faith

(Matt. 16:21-23; also 14:22-31). He is infamous in all four Gospels for his threefold denial of Jesus Christ (see Matt. 26:69-75).

But Peter was not the only apostle to misunderstand Jesus and his teaching. John and James shamelessly asked for both seats of power (Matt. 20:20-28) despite Jesus' repeated prophecies about his own suffering and death (Matt. 16:21-23; 17:22-23; 20:17-19). They, along with the other disciples, clearly misunderstood their role as followers of Christ and thereby their role as leaders. In the end, they scattered with the rest of the disciples when Jesus was arrested. One is left to wonder, *How can any of these people be leaders in the community of God?*

Case Study in Abraham

Abraham (originally Abram) is, indisputably, the father of faith for both Jews and Gentile Christians. The Israelites' national identity has its beginning in Abraham (see Gen. 12:1-3). And for Paul, Abraham is the father of not only Jews but Gentiles, since righteousness is reckoned not by law, but by faith (Gal. 3:1-29, esp. v. 29). Abraham is the father of all those who have faith, because when all hope of producing an heir was gone, he believed in the promise of God that there would be an heir from Sarah's and his own bodies (Rom. 4:18-22).

Yet Abraham was also a liar and a selfish husband. In Genesis 12:10-20, as Abram and Sarai journey to Egypt, Abram contrived to deceive the Egyptians: Abram would pass Sarai as his sister rather than his wife in order to preserve his own life (Gen. 12:11-13). Abram's plan had devastating results. As Sarai was taken to the pharaoh's house, God afflicted the household with plagues (Gen. 12:17). And Pharaoh's piercing question to Abram was not simply embarrassing but resembled God's question to Eve in the Garden of Eden: "What is this you have done to me?" (Gen. 12:18, ESV; cf. 3:13).[11] Even if one tries to explain away Abram's guilt as a sin of omission or half lie (see Gen. 20:12-13), the verbal echo of Genesis 3:13 indicates that Abram was guilty of sinful (self-preserving and duplicitous) behavior.

In Genesis 13, we see a portrait of Abram in all his weakness, a human not unlike the rest of us. Abram's journey to pagan Egypt was understandable; there was a famine in the land, but in Egypt the famine was less severe (Gen. 12:10).[12] But there, in the face of foreigners, Abram did not demonstrate courage and faith in God's promises, but fear. This fear did not concern the welfare of Sarai, but Abram himself (Gen. 12:12). And at this point, we see a little more than fear; we see Abram's selfishness. He was willing to risk the safety of Sarai to preserve his own life.[13]

Genesis 13 goes on to describe the confrontation between the pharaoh and Abram. Recall that Pharaoh's initial words echo God's words to Eve in the Garden of Eden.[14] Hence, while there was no indication of God's anger or displeasure against Abram, the echo suggests that Abram's behavior was less than exemplary. In an ironic reversal, the reprimand did not come from God but from Pharaoh. The member of the covenant was rebuked by one who was outside of God's covenant. This embarrassing turnaround has a dramatic effect on how we understand God's people, indeed God's leaders.[15]

God chooses people out of grace and mercy. God's calling is not based on human merit and inherent goodness; God calls us in spite of our thoroughly flawed nature. Abraham's case proves that. From the multiple calls on Abraham's life (see Gen. 12:1-3; 15:1-20; 17:1-27; 22:15-19), we also see that becoming the leader God calls us to be takes time; it is a process. And finally, we see that while Abram repeatedly failed, God's grace and calling endured. Failure did not eliminate God's grace and did not lead to forfeiture of God's promises. Instead, we see God's grace at work to bring Abraham to the point where he could be the father of faith.

Like these heroes of the faith, ANA leadership in the church is indeed an imperfect model of Christ's sacrificial leadership over his people. Paul writes in Romans 7:24, "What a wretched man I am! Who will rescue me from this body that is subject to death?" But he goes on to say, "Thanks be to God, who delivers me through Jesus Christ our Lord! . . . Therefore, there is now no condemnation for those who are in Christ Jesus, because through Christ Jesus the law of the Spirit who gives life has set you free from the law of sin and death" (7:25–8:2, NIV).

Through the foundation of Christ's saving grace, we are no longer bound by our past failures, fears, or cultural values. As members of God's family, we can learn to embrace our brokenness as we trust in God's redemptive purposes for the church as well as for the world. How should the biblical principles of humility and embracing our brokenness inform the way in which we develop lay leadership?

Empowerment: Creating Grace-Filled Learning Environments

The formation of servants in God's household begins as we admit our own weaknesses, fears, and failures (see Mark 1:14-15; Acts 2:37-38). As we understand the extent of our brokenness and experience the healing power of God's grace, we are slowly set free from unhealthy cultural and familial strongholds. As we forgive and experience forgiveness, we are set free not *because of* our good works, but *for* the good works God has already planned for us to do (Eph. 2:8-10).

As ANA Christians, we can experience healing from perfectionism and become free to make mistakes and learn from them. We can understand our calling to be good stewards of the resources that have been entrusted to us (see Matt. 25:14-30). We can be motivated to work hard not out of a fear of shame or failure but out of a sense of joy, gratitude, and purpose. Our leadership then becomes a reflection of God's leadership, the call to serve rather than be served, and the countercultural downward movement (Phil. 2:6-8) that leads to greater concern for others than for ourselves (Phil. 2:3-4). This kind of leadership emerges out of the call to maturity, to reconciliation, unity, and peace in the family of God (Eph. 2:11-22), and it is formed in a culture of grace.

Leadership in a Culture of Grace

We saw in the example of Abram how God's grace in the context of brokenness can shape leadership. In 1 John 3:1 we are reminded that we are loved. We are loved no matter what. We are loved so "lavishly" by God that we are invited to do whatever we see our heavenly Father doing. It is in this context of love that Christ himself is formed in us, where we grow to be spiritual adults who joyfully embrace the calling and responsibility of leadership.

New believers must be given an abundance of love and attention if they are to grow up in healthy ways. They must be invited to explore life God's way, to try new things, to attempt great things, knowing that they are not alone. A foundation of grace enables young believers to trust that God and their spiritual community are there to help them and catch them when they fall. They develop confidence in their abilities and learn that failure is just another way everyone learns and grows into maturity. Like Abraham in the book of Genesis, we can embrace our brokenness in the process of leadership development.

In 2 Timothy 2:2, Paul reminds his spiritual son that leaders lead ministries, but more importantly they have both the responsibility and privilege of raising up the next generation of leaders in the body of Christ. Paul had demonstrated this principle through his relationship with Timothy. Healthy leadership development takes place in the church when current leaders, those with power and influence, are intentional about creating a context of grace in their own spiritual households. It is in a true culture of grace that potential leaders flourish as they are invited into greater levels of leadership. Those who are willing can be invested in, mentored, empowered, and released into leadership, even as they are coached and cared for over time by more experienced leaders.

Does our church context have a culture of grace? Are members invited into deeper devotion and significant ministries? Are we helping one another attempt great things by reminding each other that we have a great God?

Invitation to Lead

In *Invitation to Lead*, Paul Tokunaga begins with the words, "I am a leader, but I was not born to lead." Tokunaga goes on to describe how the cultural values of Asian Americans often prevent them from being seen and seeing themselves as leaders.[16] In the ANA church, members will offer to help in a variety of ministries but are often unwilling to be the point person because leadership seems so daunting. In such a context, we can learn much about leadership development from Jesus.

In John 1:35-39 Jesus invited those who would later become leaders in his church to first "come and see," to observe and get to know him and how he was living his life. Then, as people got to know Jesus, his heart and character, his power and purposes, he invited them into deeper discipleship, saying in Luke 9:23, "Follow me." Those who accepted his invitation would join him in ministry, watching Jesus teach and heal, extending mercy and kindness to sinners and outcasts.

Luke 9 and 10 tell us that after a while Jesus began to send out those who had been serving with him to "preach the kingdom of God and to heal the sick" just as he had been doing. Upon their return, Jesus debriefed with them, using these opportunities for further teaching, challenges, and words of encouragement.

How can the ANA church develop a culture of leadership development in which faithful members are invited to "come and see" how experienced leaders and pastors live their lives and minister as faithfully as they can? How can potential leaders be encouraged to learn and grow with intentionality and commitment, knowing they are supported and loved as they discover their own sense of calling and ministry focus?

Begin with the invitation to come and see, to observe, and begin to engage in the ministry at hand. It is an invitation to do ministry with someone else, with the understanding that they will soon do ministry on their own as the Holy Spirit leads and guides.

A few years ago I (Nancy) took on responsibility for our struggling young adult ministry. After regrouping and building up a small core team, we looked forward to a new, exciting season of growth. We were praying for a key young adult lay leader to provide vision and leadership for this ministry. More than that, I was looking for an opportunity to invest in the next generation of believers so they could more effectively reach their peers with the good news of Jesus Christ.

As a college student leader with Campus Crusade for Christ, I was taught to look for potential leaders who were *FAT*: *f*aithful, *a*vailable, and *t*eachable. I was also looking for someone who was passionate about God, who cared about people, and who would have good chemistry with me. With God's prompting and approval by our elders, the lead pastor and I invited a faithful twenty-eight-year-old church member to quit his job and accept a full-time, paid pastoral internship overseeing our developing young adult ministry. We promised to teach him whatever we could and provide him with resources for his spiritual growth so that he could discern whether God was calling him into full-time ministry. We gave him a task to do, and I met with him weekly, challenging his thinking and values, providing counsel and guidance for his ministry.

Because this was an internship, my primary commitment to him would be to support him personally in his training and discernment process. His work in the ministry itself, though important, was secondary. The success of his time with us would not be based on the numerical or even the spiritual growth of the young adult ministry alone. It would in fact be especially dependent on how much he was able to grow in knowledge and understanding of God's heart, truth, and purposes. It would be dependent on how deeply he understood what the church was called to be about and how God might be calling him to participate in God's mission to the world. Our mutual success was dependent on the extent to which God's love and grace were transforming his own heart and the hearts of others through his leadership. So there was freedom to learn, explore, risk, and fail. This was a learning experience and not just a job.

What was expected of this young man in this role was a posture of faithfulness, integrity, humility, respect for God's Word, and submission to the leadership of the church, which included me as his immediate supervisor (Heb. 12:1-17; 13:7,17). We would decide together what his responsibilities would be and what he wanted to learn or experience. His training would include recommended classes, conferences, our mentoring relationship, and a variety of ministry experiences. We would follow the process of "I do it and you watch. We do it together. You do it and I watch." Not only would he learn ministry skills, but he would put those skills into practice right away.

I would be his primary mentor, ministry coach, and spiritual director, and invite others to provide additional mentoring. Perceived successes as well as perceived failures would all be part of the learning process. As this intern grew in competency, I would release more and more leadership to him. My ultimate goal was to completely hand over leadership and responsibility of the young adult ministry to him when he was at least 50 percent capable of handling it himself. Then I could lead from a coaching position, eventually working myself out of a job. Thus far, this has been one of the most enjoyable ministry relationships I have had.

Inviting someone to serve with you is one of the most significant aspects of leadership development. An invitation to lead in a culture of grace communicates affirmations such as, "I like you," "I believe in you," and "I would like to partner with you." Inviting someone to be part of your team in an attempt to do something significant tells that person, "Your ideas and insights are important," "We could benefit from your gifts and abilities," and "God's hand is upon you."

An invitation to lead or colead must be given without pressure or expectation to excel. Instead, this invitation must provide an opportunity for someone to learn how to be faithful to his or her gifts and calling. This kind of invitation is rarely declined, because it is an invitation of grace and generosity. At some point, the call to deeper commitment can then be made. Members can be invited (and challenged) to make greater sacrifices, not just to serve in more significant ways, but to grow and mature in character and devotion to God along the way.

Do you remember the first time someone you respected, a leader or someone in authority, asked you to join him or her in ministry?

When was the last time you affirmed the gifts and calling of someone newer to ministry and invited that person to partner with you in serving others? How committed are those in positions of influence to the development of the next generations of leaders?

Investing in the Next Generation

A well-known hospital in the San Francisco Bay Area is known as a "teaching hospital." This means that patients are not just examined by the attending physician, but by three or four interns as well. Although patient care is of primary importance, it is also important that students from the Stanford University School of Medicine receive practical experience and on-the-job training. In this instructive environment, students are exposed to real-life situations. They are challenged to address real problems, their work is supervised, and they are given honest and timely feedback to help them develop as physicians. What would it look like if every church were a "teaching" church?

Potential leaders should understand that they begin in leadership as students, not experts. They are not expected to do everything perfectly the first time. They are not expected to lead a Bible study group or a short-term mission team as though they have been leading for years. Instead, potential leaders *must* believe that they are members of a grace-filled household and that it is okay to fail and fail often, especially when they are attempting to follow in the steps of Jesus. And it is up to the more experienced leaders to communicate and affirm this message of grace in both word and deed.

Years ago, when I (Nancy) was first learning to ski, a friend of mine who was an expert skier spent time helping me improve. He would watch as I attempted steeper hills and often found myself falling out of control. At times I would get frustrated, wrestling with feelings of inadequacy and defeat. My friend would call out from across the hill, "Remember, if you're not falling, you're not learning!" Falling meant that I was challenging myself by attempting what was beyond my current ability. My friend would then offer a suggestion or two before skiing away. His words gave me encouragement and also spurred me on to make some much-needed adjustments. It is often in our failures that we are the most teachable, appreciative of encouragement, and most open to feedback or advice.

As experienced leaders, we *must* be willing to allow younger leaders and ministries to flounder at times. In ANA families, when a son or daughter does not perform well, it is the parents who bear the burden of shame or judgment in the community. Likewise, pastors and senior leaders can sometimes be more concerned with our own image than with the development of younger leaders. We offer these exhortations to experienced leaders who are committed to the leadership development process:

- Look beyond the inevitable failures to the potential for personal growth these failures can bring.

- Don't be afraid of how the failures of inexperienced leaders will be attributed to them.

- Resist reacting to false judgments; instead, uphold the value of grace and humility within the church.

- Release control and allow younger leaders to learn and grow through their failures as well as their successes.

- Be willing to give honest and constructive feedback as well as encouragement on a regular basis.

When developing new small-group leaders, elders, or ministry team leaders, how can senior leaders create a culture of learning and growing, rather than a culture of performance and perfection? How can experienced leaders see themselves as equippers of other leaders, making it a priority to grow in their own ability to teach and train others? How can the church become more like a teaching hospital, training church members to grow in character and faithfulness even as they grow in ministry competence?

Soul Care and Ministry Competency

One of the greatest challenges of developing leaders is the willingness of experienced leaders to be vulnerable about our own weaknesses and failures. This humility reflects an important value of the household of God that we develop from the book of Philippians. In shame-based ANA cultures, many senior leaders are unwilling to dispel the false image of self-determination and perfectionism in order to retain the ensuing effects of honor and respect in their churches. But this false image creates an unachievable model of perfection for potential leaders and hinders their authenticity. At the same time, the more they are involved in ministry, the more potential leaders will begin to see the weaknesses of those in authority. Without opportunities for humble confession and forgiveness, the church falls prey to distrust, resentment, and even disillusionment.

Experienced leaders are as much in need of constant development and grace as younger leaders. Ephesians 2:21-22 reminds us that the health and growth of every member is dependent on those around them, whether they are younger or older, experienced or passionate, reflective or active. In fact, it is often when we commit ourselves to forming deep relationships with those who are not like ourselves that our character and heart are most transformed. And indeed, the power of God is manifested not in strength, but in weakness (2 Cor. 12:9). When we are honest about our weaknesses, we may lose the honor and respect that are based on cultural values, but we will gain the power of God.

Perhaps as much as any disciple of Christ, the apostle Paul had reason to boast in his own righteousness. Though he refrained from such boasting, God gave him "a thorn in [the] flesh" to keep him humble. "Three times I pleaded with the Lord to take it away from me," Paul admitted. But God told him, "My grace is sufficient for you, for my power is made perfect in weakness." "Therefore," Paul declared, "I will boast all the more gladly about my weaknesses, so that Christ's power may rest on me. . . . For when I am weak, then I am strong" (2 Cor. 12:6-10, NIV).

God works through our humility and weaknesses. The ministry that any church leader is called to, whether old or young, is one based on grace and not merit. As Paul clearly states, all of us fall short of the glory of God, but through Christ there is grace for all (Rom. 3:23-26). Then, as Paul appropriately asks in Romans 3:27,

"Where, then, is boasting?" We can all agree with Paul, "It is excluded" (NIV). How refreshing it would be if ANA church leaders could model this understanding of God's grace in their ministry not only for future leaders, but for all congregation members.

The Lighthouse Christian Church identifies itself as a "small groups" church. This means that we encourage everyone to commit to being part of a smaller group of six to ten individuals who meet weekly in people's homes. Small group members extend mutual care and encouragement, study God's Word, and commit to serving one another and the world together. Although many of these groups develop a strong sense of community over time, group members often remain reluctant to share deeper personal struggles because of feelings of shame and failure.

Last year we began to encourage members to commit to meeting weekly in even smaller accountability groups with only one or two others. These more intimate "life transformation" groups provided greater confidentiality, which encouraged more honest sharing, prayer, and accountability for both group members and leaders. Everyone on our pastoral staff committed to joining life transformation groups as well as communicating a greater sense of mutuality and authenticity to the church.

My (Nancy's) own accountability partnerships have given me a place to share personal struggles with a couple of people who have developed into those I can truly call my friends. Although there must be sensitivity in revealing issues in the church, as leaders we must seek opportunities to model mutuality, confession, and transparency to those around us. It is only when leaders are recipients of God's grace that we can be entrusted to extend God's grace to others. When we humble ourselves in times of honest confession, we live out God's calling of unity and maturity in the household of God.

Ephesians 4:15 says that it is in "speaking the truth in love" that everyone in the household of God will build each other up in love. This context of grace and mutuality is critical when providing and receiving feedback regarding ministry and leadership competence. Experienced leaders must provide regular opportunities to give loving but honest feedback to those on their staff. They must learn how to speak truth in love with the goal of exhorting and building up one another (Eph. 4:15-16). In the same way, senior leaders must also create regular opportunities to invite and receive honest feedback themselves. They must learn to model humility and encourage authenticity in their own personal life and leadership. As they do so, younger leaders will grow up in environments where humble and mutual exhortation is the norm. They will learn that mistakes or failures are part of the growth and development of all leaders.

Are younger leaders given regular times of grace-filled personal and ministry feedback? Do experienced leaders provide opportunities for receiving honest and constructive criticisms themselves? Is every leader committed to mutual submission and the kind of personal growth that occurs only through honest confession and loving exhortation?

Cultivating Leadership Vision

Jesus says to his disciples in John 14:12, "Very truly I tell you, whoever believes in me will do the works I have been doing, and they will do even greater things than these" (NIV). One of the challenges of developing ANA lay leaders is to help them discover God's calling in their lives. Most of these leaders have grown up learning how to please their parents, teachers, and even their pastors. So when they are invited into positions of leadership, they find it difficult to develop a clear vision for themselves or their own generation.

As we have previously observed, first-generation immigrants sometimes pursue positions of leadership in the church as a way to obtain the status and respect denied to them in mainstream society. But second-generation leaders are often not interested in leadership positions at all. Instead, they struggle with apathy and worldly pursuits that distract them from God and his purposes. They do not see the church as an agent of change in the world, or at least not a powerful one.

Like Jessica in our opening illustrations, sometimes their attempts at taking initiative have resulted in dismissal by ministry gatekeepers or have failed to affect significant change. So before they will step into leadership, these young leaders must first embrace a new vision of God's kingdom purposes. Then they must be given the opportunity to make significant changes not just within the church but in their community outside the church walls. They must be captivated by the hope of the gospel to transform the brokenness in their own lives as well as the brokenness in the world.

Often the vision for a hope-filled future will not look the same for different members of a church family. In his book *True Story*, James Choung describes our mission in life as being "sent together to heal" our world, restoring it to the way God originally designed it to be. This vision of a world "designed for good" is what the kingdom of God is supposed to look like. But for a new generation of young adults, this picture of a world characterized by justice and compassion for all is much more compelling than mere personal salvation.[17]

Second- and third-generation leaders will need to identify and develop their own calling and vision for ministry to their peers. Not only must they be given the opportunity to envision their own ministry direction, but they must be given wise counsel and resources to help them clarify and communicate God's hope-filled future for their own generation.

When I (Nancy) began overseeing our young adult ministry, I realized that many of our young career-age members were disconnected from each other. My passion was evangelism, and my heart ached for the many twenty- and thirtysomethings who lived and worked right in our community but did not know the saving grace of Jesus Christ. Because our own young adult group was not yet unified, they were not in a good position to reach out to their unchurched peers. So I began to gather our young adults together through dinners and community activities. I challenged our small core team to see the opportunities for evangelism and to reflect on God's call on their lives to transform their generation for Christ.

One day I asked our leadership team what would bring their unchurched friends and coworkers out to a church-sponsored event on Saturday night. They didn't know. So I asked what would bring *them* to a church gathering on a Saturday night. One leader finally spoke up and said, "I would come out to a place where people were passionate about God, where it was obvious that they loved one another, and where everyone had a clear desire to transform their world. I would want to be part of a community like that." So I said, "Great! How can we create that kind of community experience for our unchurched friends?" Their response surprised me. They replied, "But Pastor Nancy, *we* don't have that. That's what *we* want!"

I realized that if this gathering was going to be embraced by this leadership team, it wasn't going to be about what *I* wanted or envisioned, but what *they* wanted and envisioned. So we took a step back and worked with the group to clarify their vision. As we gathered together over the next three months, the Holy Spirit spoke to us, and a dozen members interested in leadership stepped up to become the core team. Together we (mostly, they) developed a clear mission statement, and the young adults all were excited about the direction and vision God had given them to become a "passionate community of young career adults who reflect God's abundant love through vibrant worship, radical faith, and selfless service" with the hope of transforming their generation with the good news of Jesus Christ.

Before our official launch, this young leadership team asked if our pastoral staff and elders would bless them and their ministry. So we invited them, along with other key leaders, for a time of fellowship, prayer, and worship. It was an amazing gathering as those in senior leadership blessed and committed to serve the younger generation. And these experienced leaders were faithful to their commitments, providing childcare and helping the young adults learn to set up the chairs, sound system, and food. Some of these leaders even prayed during the gatherings, interceding for the speakers and participants in a back room. The young adult group grew from a dozen to more than sixty members, with over a hundred attending the monthly worship gatherings each month. This display of selfless service by experienced leaders left an indelible mark on the minds and hearts of these younger leaders.

Potential leaders need experienced leaders to invest in their personal and ministry development. This investment includes not only the pastor's time and energy, but also resources from other key church leaders. Most of all, young leaders need encouragement to develop their own vision by listening to God's voice and relying on the power of God's Holy Spirit in grace-filled households.

The Urgency of Developing Servants in God's Household

Much of what I [Nancy] learned about Christ-centered leadership development came from my years as a student in college campus ministry. Looking back, there were basically three phases in our ministry. The first phase began with joining a small group of like-minded Christ followers who were being mentored by a Christian leader for our spiritual growth. The second phase included meeting one-on-one with a leader for personal and spiritual mentoring. In the third phase, we were considered leaders and focused our time on reaching out to help spiritually (and often physically) younger students grow and give their lives more deeply to Jesus. There wasn't much time to relax or coast. Every year we were expected to move from one phase to another, from a young believer to a spiritual leader—even at the ripe old age of twenty-one! Our college years were limited, so there was a sense of urgency to grow and lead and then raise up leaders to take our place. After graduation, as I became a young career person and joined my neighborhood church, I noticed that this sense of urgency did not seem to exist outside the college campus.

Has the church lost its sense of focus and mission to be fruitful and multiply? Are we caught up in the building of larger churches and bigger budgets such that we have neglected to prioritize the raising up of leaders, pastors, and church planters?

The apostle Paul spent about ten years of his life planting churches around the Roman Empire. He did not stay at these churches but left their leadership in the hands of those he mentored, such as Timothy and Titus. Paul had invited them into a mentoring relationship with him that included teaching, service together, counseling, and exhortations. Perhaps he knew his time on this earth was to be short-lived. Perhaps he understood the importance of investing his life into those who would be able to mentor others. Paul was not a perfect man by any means, but he was faithful and honest about his weaknesses and failures. Those he loved and mentored became his spiritual family, and through them the nations were blessed by God.

As pastors and leaders, what priority will we give in the development and formation of God's servants in his household? How can and will we pay attention to our own lives and become grace-filled leaders who set the tone for grace-filled ministry? God calls each of us to invest our lives well and then look forward to the fruit that God will bear through the lives that we love and nurture in Jesus' name.

✦
NOTES

1. Jonathan Y. Tan, *Introducing Asian American Theologies* (Maryknoll, NY: Orbis, 2008), 59–62, 69–70.

2. Ibid., 10–11, 37–39.

3. See also Galatians 1:13-16 and 2 Corinthians 11:22.

4. I. Howard Marshall, *The Epistle to the Philippians*, Epworth Commentaries (London: Epworth, 1991), 50–51.

5. The word usually translated "servant" is *doulos*, meaning "slave."

6. Moises Silva, *Philippians*, 2nd ed. Baker Exegetical Commentary on the New Testament (Grand Rapids: Baker Academic, 2005), 86–88.

7. Markus Bockmuehl, *The Epistle to the Philippians*, Black's New Testament Commentary (London: A. & C. Black, 1997), 175.

8. In the Greek text, the word translated "serve" in 2:22 is *edouleusen;* aorist tense of the verb *douleu* "to serve as a slave." It contains the same root as *doulos*, the Greek term for "slave."

9. The verb *kauchaomai* can be translated either "to boast" or "to glory oneself."

10. See Bockmuehl, *Philippians*, 192.

11. A. P. Ross, *Creation and Blessing: A Guide to the Study and Exposition of Genesis* (Grand Rapids: Baker, 1998), 277.

12. There is no prohibition to this journey from God, so there is no need to interpret this journey as something against God's will.

13. At this point, we can explore some interpretive options for Abram's behavior. Positively, while Abram had no intentions of harm toward Sarai, he was guilty of not thinking clearly. Consumed by fear, he did not consider the possible outcome of his actions. Negatively, we might see Abram as not

only a coward, but as a selfish man concerned only with saving his own skin. Perhaps Abram had interpreted God's calling in Genesis 12 as one that only applied to him and not Sarai. However we interpret Abram's actions here, Abram would repeat this behavior in Genesis 20:1-18, where his innocence and naïveté become more difficult to sustain. Abram's ruse seems to have been habitual (Gen. 20:13).

14. V. P. Hamilton, *The Book of Genesis: Chapters 1-17*, NICOT (Grand Rapids: Eerdmans, 1990), 385. Hamilton's words are incisive: "In fact, Pharaoh exemplifies a higher degree of moral sensitivity than does the patriarch."

15. Ross, *Creation*, 272: "Israel would learn that, even when they were unfaithful, there were aspects of the promise that God would not relinquish through their failure. This deliverance in no way condoned the deception; rather, it embarrassed it."

16. Paul Tokunaga, *Invitation to Lead* (Downers Grove, IL: InterVarsity, 2003), 52–60.

17. James Choung, *True Story: A Christianity Worth Believing In* (Downers Grove, IL: InterVarsity, 2008), 195–200.

CHAPTER 8

✝

Children of Light
Following Jesus in Public Life

TIMOTHY TSENG
AND JONATHAN WU

Fresh from their honeymoon, Anthuan and Sue Nguyen enter the church building with their faces aglow. During the sermon, several people steal affectionate glances at the blushing young newlyweds. The fellowship at the Vietnamese church in San Jose, California, is intimate and comfortable. Like their peers, Anthuan and Sue are upwardly mobile American-born children of refugees from the Vietnam War. They are college educated and have jobs that pay well. Having just purchased a new home, Anthuan and Sue are on the path to their American dream. They epitomize the aspirations of many Vietnamese American families who seek to overcome the trauma of war and displacement.

On this particular morning, however, Anthuan and Sue are unusually focused on the sermon, despite their friends' efforts to distract them. For some reason, the fresh-out-of-seminary pastor's challenge to love their neighbors strikes a nerve. Later that day, when a jobless and homeless African American family approach them outside a restaurant, Anthuan and Sue invite them to their home for a meal. Touched by the family's stories of struggle, the newlywed couple sets them up in a hotel and invites them to church. Pastor Tran embraces them warmly, the rest of the church less so. But everyone prays earnestly and sincerely for the new family to get back on its feet. The church's young adults share the gospel with the teenage sons of the family in hopes that they will accept Christ. Collections are taken to help buy the family new clothing and pay for rent.

After a month, the Nguyens become frustrated. They cannot afford to continue paying for the family's rent. The teens are not going to school. The parents refuse to enter a homeless shelter and are not actively searching for work. In fact, they begin asking church members for money. Once tight-knit and comfortable, the mood at the church becomes increasingly tense. None of the younger people want to be viewed as racists, but they start to harbor stereotypical images of African Americans. Some even openly express their dislike of the family. Even Pastor Tran is puzzled—loving one's neighbors is not that easy!

At last Pastor Tran and the Nguyens decide that they can no longer sustain this codependent relationship. The church stops paying the rent. The family is told that they are welcome at the church but can no longer ask the members for money. The family is also referred to a social worker. The family does not return to the church.

Anthuan and Sue, Pastor Tran, and most church members are disappointed but relieved. As they reflect on what they have experienced, they realize that loving one's neighbor requires much more than they had anticipated. It demands more than simply offering help and meeting practical needs. Outside the church is a public where rich and poor; men and women; black, white, Asian, and Hispanic; religious and secular occupy distinct spheres that coexist but rarely engage with one another. And even though Anthuan, Sue, and their peers spend time in different public settings each day, their faith's greatest impact is in the private religious sphere of the church. Bringing Christ into work, the economy, family life, community service, political involvement, or even leisure and recreation is a daunting task.

Asian North American (ANA) Christians and the Challenge of Public Life

ANA Christianity has had a presence in North America since the seventeenth century, when a Catholic Filipino community settled in the part of Spanish America that is known today as Louisiana.

Chinese and Japanese settlements in nineteenth-century Hawaii and early twentieth-century United States were often perceived as a dubious foreign presence by most Americans—this, despite the fact that many Asian American spokespersons were Christian clergy.[1] Today, judging from most media accounts, many still perceive ANA Christians as disinterested or unengaged in public life. Their congregations seem to lack leaders who articulate coherent public theologies that link core beliefs and values to visible and transformative practices. While this may be true for immigrant ANA Christians who arrived after 1965 and for their children, it does not accurately describe the generation of ANA Christians who came of age after World War II. Indeed, many Japanese, Chinese, and Korean Protestants and Filipino Catholics brought their faith into public life.

For example, during the Sino-Japanese War and World War II, Chinese Christians mobilized their community to support China and to end racially discriminatory immigration laws. Japanese *Nisei* Christians, stung by their World War II internment camp experiences, were energized to fight for civil rights and redress. Catholic Filipinos allied themselves with Philip Vera Cruz and Caesar Chavez to fight for farm workers' rights. Many prominent ANA educators, community activists, public servants, actors, and artists in the 1960s and 1970s grew up in ANA mainline Protestant churches where public engagement was encouraged.[2]

The majority of ANA churches today, however, were planted by post-1965 immigrants who did not share the immediate post–World War II ANA congregational experience. They and their children were disconnected from these faith communities and were, instead, more greatly influenced by the fundamentalist, evangelical, and Pentecostal movements in Asia and North America. Many recognized the importance of living out the gospel of Jesus in all of life, but because they found themselves at the margins of North American life, they faced obstacles that thwarted such convictions to take root in their shared life and witness. Their children also were rarely exposed to a Christian faith that encouraged public engagement. So, the question is, why? What happened to ANA Christianity between the pre-1965 and post-1965 generations?

Before we discuss the factors that block ANA public engagement, let's first discuss what "public life" means.

What Is Public Life?

The public sphere is generally defined as the arena of life in which one interacts with people outside one's family, where business is transacted, and where news is transmitted from one group to another. The private sphere is traditionally limited to the home or kinship group, limited to relationships formed by biological ties or legal covenants (marriage, adoption). In Scripture, for example, Joseph, upon learning that his fiancée, Mary, was pregnant, wanted to divorce her privately and avoid exposing her to "public" disgrace (Matt. 1:19). Jesus withdrew from the public to a private place by himself or with his disciples for prayer and renewal (e.g., Matt. 14:13; Luke 5:16; John 6:15).

All human beings inhabit both public and private spheres to one degree or another. In various seasons in history, the lines between the two have blurred and crystallized. At times, depending on one's perceptions, there appear to be gaps between the spheres that widen and narrow. Various questions have sparked controversy: What is the appropriate sphere for men, for women, for children? What is the appropriate place for religion? What is the appropriate relationship between religion and government, between church and state, between faith and politics? Should government be empowered to regulate religion? Should one's personal religious convictions be permitted to legislate the choices of others?

The public or private divide clearly existed in the premodern world. But in modern industrialized societies, the gap between public and private increased tremendously. The public has become the arena where we work to sustain ourselves, where we create and shape national culture, and where we debate public policy and engage in politics. The private sphere has become the place where our families, religious communities, and convictions, moral values, and individual preferences and hobbies are sequestered and sustained.

In most democratic nations today, religion is deemed a private matter. This principle of separation of church and state protects freedom of religion while guarding against oppressive theocracy. Yet the extent to which government can regulate religion for the common good or to which religious interests can participate in politics remains greatly debated. Similarly, the extent to which religious expressions can be displayed in public often engenders perspectives that range from complete prohibition of any religious displays to the hodgepodge celebration of all religions. To what extent should Christian convictions and values be publicly displayed today?

This chapter assumes that Christians, particularly ANA Christians, *should* engage public life. We do not suggest the elimination of the dividing line between public and private spheres. Indeed, we would consider excessive the governmental regulation of religion and private affairs in many Asian countries where the public/private divide is even less clear-cut than in North America.

At the same time, we find it encouraging that increased numbers of ANA Christian leaders are exploring the meaning of public discipleship. As we saw in Pastor Tran and the Nguyens' experience, it is often difficult to put these convictions into practice. Nevertheless, a theology that focuses on personal evangelism and caring ministries without taking into account social structures and power dynamics will not bring about lasting change or sustain the faith commitment and hard work of the believers. Since post-1965 ANA congregations tend to focus on sustaining the private lives of their own people; few have considered the kind of positive roles they can play in their communities and in public policy.

What factors have led ANA Christians to avoid their calling to participate in the public sphere in the name of Christ? We identify three critical obstacles appear to contribute to the impoverishment of public faith and life in post-1965 ANA Christianity: a more privatized religion, racial exclusion and marginality, and a disconnected theological inheritance.

A More Privatized Religion

Christianity is still the dominant religion in North America today. In two 2008 US-based surveys, a little over three-quarters of Americans identify themselves as Christians. This, however, represents a drop of roughly 10 percent since 1990. One might assume that the recent growth of immigration from non-Christian countries caused this decline. But the percentage of *non*-Christian religions in America has grown only between .5 and 1.5 percent between 1990 and 2008. The group that has grown the most has been those who are "not religious" (from 8.2 percent to between 15 and 16 percent).[3] Most in this category are young adults.

What is happening? Is there a widespread negative reaction to the political activism of the so-called Religious Right? Perhaps. But more likely it is the culmination of an anti-institutional attitude that has been growing since the 1960s. As early as 1985, sociologist Robert Bellah identified an increasing personal worldview that he called "Sheilaism" in his classic study, *Habits of the Heart*. "Sheila" was raised in the Christian church, but rather than embracing those beliefs in adulthood, she created her own religious identity out of different religions and pursued a satisfying life without institutional religion. For more than a generation now, the fastest-growing population has been the tribe of "Sheilaism," the church of "spiritual, but not religious."[4]

The turn to disconnected and individualistic spirituality is part of the trend that views faith as a private affair. Faith has application only to personal well-being and has little to say about family life, community, social issues, and politics. Some social scientists, such as Robert D. Putnam, see increased individualism and privatization as reasons for "the collapse of social capital" in North American society.[5] Television and the Internet are blamed for keeping people home rather than participating in community life (including church attendance). Fewer North Americans participate in traditional community activities, such as bowling leagues, local political clubs, or neighborhood churches. Without vibrant participation in community and public life, Putnam and Bellah fear a weakening of democracy that could undermine the health of North American institutions.

We do not completely agree with Putnam and Bellah. Individualism has been central to the North American narrative. Historians note that each generation has reported the loss of community and participation in public life in the face of rapid social change. Many scholars believe that increased individualism and privatization does not change the basic human need for community and public life. What has changed is *how* people build community and engage public life (e.g., online social networking, blogging, and Twitter). Many theologians point to the "emerging church" with its postmodern sensitivities as an example of how a new generation of Christians are reengaging community and public life.

"Progressive" Christians, represented by Jim Wallis and the Sojourners community and mainline Protestantism, continue to engage public life on traditional peace and social justice issues. The Religious Right, led by the Family Research Council, also engage the public but focus on social issues that strike many Americans as "private morality." Yet surveys indicate that, despite left- and right-wing Christian activism, religion for most Americans today, including ANAs, is increasingly viewed as a private matter that ought to remain disconnected from public life. Thus, the lack of ANA engagement into public life can be attributed, in part, to a broad sentiment that a person's religious convictions should be hidden.

Racial Exclusion and Marginality

Another important factor that prevents ANA Christians from engaging public life is their experience of racial exclusion and marginality.[6] This may seem odd for people who do not think the ANA population faces discrimination. Indeed, most post-1965 ANA Christians have benefited from the dismantling of racial barriers in public life thanks largely to the civil rights movement. ANA achievements in education and economics are touted as evidence that they are more like European immigrants than African Americans. The experience of racism is therefore not considered as real for ANA "model minorities" who seem to be able to advance without governmental intervention or other special initiatives.

Furthermore, many Asian ethnic groups resist being labeled Asian Americans (or Asian Canadians) because these terms were imposed on them. They want to remain tethered to their unique experiences as Chinese, Korean, Filipino, and so on. Some even question the merits of using Asian American (or Asian North American,

Asian and Pacific Islander American, etc.) as a useful racial category. It is then implied that because some Asians experience greater economic and educational discrimination than other Asians, race is not an adequate way to measure discrimination.

Thus, many ANA Christians do not see the ANA community itself as a focus for public engagement. Instead, ANA Christian leaders tend to "leapfrog" the ANA community in order to engage mainstream North American public issues or global mission causes. For example, Pastor Tran's challenge would be to prioritize the homeless in his congregation's neighborhood, the Vietnamese American community, or the work in Vietnam. If he and his congregation believe that Vietnamese Americans are model minorities, then ANA concerns would be overlooked.

Contrary to perceptions about ANAs as the model minority who have overcome discrimination, the reality is not so rosy. Racial equality cannot be measured by educational and economic attainment alone. Citizenship and the sense of belonging in North America are at the heart of any conversation about race and ANAs. These distinguish the history of anti-ANA discrimination from that of African-, Latino-, and, to a lesser degree, Native North Americans. For most of the nineteenth and twentieth centuries, Asians, regardless of national origin, were perceived as so utterly foreign that cultural integration into white America was considered impossible. This idea justified the passage of laws that prohibited Asians from entering, gaining citizenship, and purchasing property in late-nineteenth and early-twentieth-century United States and Canada. It was the rationale for forcibly relocating 120,000 Japanese Americans (half of whom were US citizens) to internment camps during World War II.

The more open-minded, which included many white Protestants, entertained the notion that American-born children of Asian immigrants could be assimilated once they give up their foreignness (their accent, cultural heritage, and religion). Anything "Oriental," even among the second generation, had no place on American soil. While these ideas may be fading today, there remains a huge legacy of literature, scholarship, and popular culture that find its way into North American media and institutional practices. The sense of "foreignness" also continues to feed stereotypes of martial arts misfits, inept Asian leadership (the nerd) in public settings, and the desire of Asian women to "trade up" by marrying white men in order to "fit into" American society.[7]

Because racial discrimination is so subtle in the twenty-first century, ANAs are not always conscious of being marginalized. Many ANAs compensate for that unspoken feeling of marginalization by mercilessly driving themselves toward educational and economic success. Perhaps they subconsciously believe that public recognition will reduce the discomfort. Some blame the perfectionist culture of their immigrant parents for their tireless work ethic. But blaming perfectionism only reinforces the "model minority" stereotype and diminishes the role of racial discrimination when confronted with the "bamboo ceiling" in public life.[8]

ANA Christians respond to this subtle discrimination in a variety of ways. The "silent exodus" of disillusioned young adults and the push in many ANA congregations to become multiracial are responses that have received much attention. At first glance, the departure of young adults from ANA immigrant congregations and the efforts to become multiracial can be seen as solutions to racial marginalization. Many ANA Christians join multiracial or dominant culture churches, because by doing so, they feel more attuned to the biblical mandate to share and live out the gospel across cultural boundaries (see Matt. 28:16-20; Acts 1:6-8). There may also be a sense of satisfaction from publicly demonstrating that Christian faith is able to cut against the grain of racial segregation.

Those who participate in the silent exodus and multiracial movements may actually exacerbate the racial marginalization of ANAs. As mentioned earlier, ANAs are viewed as a race of foreigners who cannot blend into North American society as easily as the children of European immigrants. Few non-Asian congregations will call ANA pastors in the foreseeable future. Where will ANA church leaders come from then? If all the young adults in Pastor Tran's congregation leave to attend non-Asian churches, there will be inadequate resources to raise up and equip ANA pastors. If Pastor Tran's congregation tries to become multiracial, it will not likely create staff positions for ANA church leaders. In the end, there may be fewer opportunities to develop ANA leadership.

Those who choose to stay in ANA churches may feel marginalized in public life. They therefore seek acceptance in the private comforts of ethnic immigrant and pan-Asian American congregations. They prefer to navigate the cultural and generational diversities within these churches than to wrestle with the subtle discrimination outside. It is unfortunate that ethnic- and race-specific congregations are not treated with great favor by many public-minded Christians. In fact, the intergenerational and cross-cultural skills required to partici-pate in these congregations are more often utilized in these churches than in multiracial churches. Ironically, the ethnic- and race-specific churches that are more closely engaged with their respective com-munities may contribute more to engaging ANA Christians to pub-lic life than multiracial churches. In the latter, ANA Christians are usually a minority and don't often engage public issues of concern to ANA communities. Ethnic Asian churches, on the other hand, usu-ally have a stronger connection with churches in Asia and are better positioned to participate in the global church.

The experience of racial marginalization is a major obstacle to ANA Christian engagement into public life. But active participation in congregations, whether ANA or multiracial, offers the greater promise for Christian public engagement than any other activity, provided that great care is taken to address the sensitive topic of race and the ANA experience. As influential as public celebrities and bloggers are (and there ought to be more who are ANA Christians), it is still the shared life within the body of Christ that will enable ANA Christians to engage public witness and discipleship. Much depends on the ability of ANA Christian leaders to overcome a third obstacle, the legacy of a theological blip.

A Disconnected Theological Inheritance

Most ANA Christian leaders today receive their theological training from evangelical seminaries. As a result, they have inherited evangel-ical and Pentecostal traditions that are ill-equipped to engage public life. While these traditions stand squarely in theological orthodoxy, their emphases and attitudes were largely formed in battle against "modernism" or liberalism in seminaries and the mission fields in the early twentieth century. In the course of that battle, the baby of a faith-based commitment to social justice and public engagement got tossed out with the "liberal-modern" bathwater.

A brief overview of the liberal-evangelical controversy sets the stage. In the modern era, an antisupernatural sentiment began to influence late-nineteenth-century Christianity in England and North America. These modern scholars did not deny the existence of God, but the Bible was seen as an historical artifact of flawed humans, and they rejected the virgin birth and the possibility of Jesus' physical resurrection and return. Conservative evangelicals responded with five fundamental beliefs as essential to orthodoxy—inerrancy of Scripture, Christ's virgin birth, substitutionary atonement, bodily resurrection, and physical return.[9]

In the same era, however, many late-nineteenth-century evangelicals began to introduce social work, education, and medical care into mission work. The social gospel movement was born to challenge the inhumane urban social conditions created by industrialization. Not all of these activists were theological "modernists," but they were condemned as such by fundamentalists who emphasized individual conversion in the mission field.[10]

Fundamentalists wrestled with modernists and social gospel advocates for control of North American seminaries and mission agencies in the 1920s and 1930s and lost. After their unhappy separation from mainline Protestantism, fundamentalists formed their own seminaries, denominations, and mission agencies—the organizations that have trained the majority of today's ANA leaders.[11]

In retrospect, the fundamentalist turn away from public engagement was a short blip in the history of American Christianity. Sandwiched around it were Christians who were vibrantly engaged in public life. The Puritans, the first and second Great Awakenings, the civil rights and antiwar movements, and contemporary progressive and conservative Christian movements are just a few examples. Indeed, most pre-1965 ANA church leaders were mainline Protestants, and they considered the engagement of public life as central to living out one's faith. But post-1965 ANA leaders would have none of that. Instead, they have inherited and passed along a theological legacy that was not accustomed to public witness.

We are not suggesting that the fundamentalist-evangelical "blip" was uniformly bad. It was a necessary detour for the recovery and renewal of global Christianity in the late twentieth century. But as this tradition comes of age and is entrusted with greater responsibility for advancing God's kingdom, it is time to engage renewed reflection on the meaning of public witness for the twenty-first century. ANA Christians should also be ready to rethink what they have inherited.

A Reconnected Theology: The Exilic Household of God

How should the ANA church, then, see her role in society and its immediate context? This question penetrates to the heart of the present dilemma for many of these congregations today. While they have served as safe havens for bringing people of similar racial backgrounds and ethnic affinities together for social, cultural, and spiritual benefits, these churches are challenged to envision themselves as intentional faith communities engaging the gospel of Jesus Christ in all of life. One critical resource in this emergence is the formation of a theology of public life. This kind of work is critical for the shaping and development of a cogent yet balanced understanding of the Christian identity in the world, expressed in the various spheres of public living.[12] This section examines key theological convictions and suggests the beginnings of a social ethics for ANA Christians.

A Good Creation

A theology of public life is anchored in the biblical foundation of creation. The Genesis account affirms that all of life, as intended by God, was created "good" (Gen. 1). The brilliance of general revelation highlights the signature of divine blessing on the full spectrum of nature and human activity. So whether it is marriage and family life, education and recreation, economics and government, or art and culture, each sphere of life bears intrinsic marks of God-created beauty and goodness.

Humans, in similar fashion, possess the image of God. Women and men, as asserted in Genesis, were formed by the breath and life of God and endowed with reflections of divine characteristics (Gen. 1:27-28; 2:7). They were placed in the midst of the created world and called to take care of and be responsible for all dimensions of life (Gen. 1:28). This would include harmonious and healthy relationships with others and faithful stewardship of God's created order. God intended people to live, play, love, work, rest, and worship. This encompassed the broad range of public life, as previously described. The doctrine of Creation highlights that everything people do becomes a living expression of faith in and faithfulness to God in God's wide and wonderful world.

God in Creation and Incarnation

A theology of public life also recognizes the centrality of God over all of creation. This is established in two ways: first, through the incarnation of Jesus and, second, through Jesus' redemptive and reconciliatory work. The Gospels reveal God present with and living among humanity in the person of Jesus (Matt. 1:23; John 1:9-11). Jesus shared and participated in all spheres of public life. He was nurtured in and connected to family (see Matt. 1:18-22; 2:11,13-15,19-23). He practiced faith and faithfulness within his community. He identified and embodied his vocation, the fullness of personal meaning and purpose. He related to the diverse worlds of business, education, government, and religion. Life was not compartmentalized into private and public. Rather, Jesus modeled a divine affirmation of the whole of life.

In addition, Jesus' death and resurrection confirmed God's sovereign rule over all creation. In his address to the Ephesians, Paul highlighted the resurrection of Christ as the affirmation of Christ's supremacy over all (1:19-23; also Col. 1:15-20). This affirmation was not only applicable to the fledgling community of his followers, but also to the existing structures of power and authority (Eph. 1:20-23). For Paul, Jesus was Lord of all. Every dimension was subject to his presence or to his preeminence. As ANA congregations wrestle with formulating a coherent theology of public life, this conviction is central. They must regard God as central to public life and so follow through on this belief. This will shape and form their identity within the community in which they reside. This will impact their communal life with respect to service, witness, and mission. This will also reflect faith and faithfulness into the workplace, home, schools, and other social settings. Engagement in a theology of public life is rooted in the creation and redemption of all of life.

Light in Darkness

The reality is that Christian faith and faithfulness today are tested and challenged by the alienating and destructive powers of darkness. Every human sphere has been tainted and ravaged by sin and evil. The rule of Christ, then, is battled and resisted. A theological social ethics is commonly marginalized or ignored, assaulted or rejected. Thus, a theology of public life must also encompass the biblical image of people of light. The letter to the Ephesians depicts the cosmic struggle between the forces of darkness and light. Paul warns that the spiritual conflict is far deeper than human and personal but involves more transcendent realities of evil, injustice, and violence (Eph. 6:10-18).

These principalities of darkness stand in opposition to the church. As Paul declares, Christians are to live as children of light (Eph. 5:8). This image of the household of God (Eph. 2:19) reiterates that the church is formed, loved, and empowered by the grace of God in order to reside in the world and to emanate the light of God through its distinctive life, service, and witness together. Paul asserts that the children of light are to expose the deeds of darkness and to live wisely (Eph. 5:11,15). Thus, there is an essential conviction that the Christian life is serious business, requiring a clear vision, resilient courage, and a passion for genuine transformation in the world.

Followers of Jesus stand in liminality. While Christians retain our identification as citizens of this world, we also uphold our residency of a heavenly realm (Phil. 3:20). We are children of God, but also people of the earth. This is best expressed in remembering our exilic identity—as a people who are not only citizens, but also strangers and foreigners (1 Pet. 2:11). Being people on the margins does not absolve Christians from fully engaging public life. In fact, even as the Israelites understood their journey as pilgrims in search of the Promised Land and later as expatriates removed from this land, they were called to seek and propagate peace and well-being wherever they were (Jer. 29:4-7). So ANA congregations are to adopt a similar disposition and venture into our corporate call as exilic households of God in their context. This is not merely an invitation to public life and witness in the increasingly multiethnic landscape of North America; it is also to elevate the level of reflection and discourse within these churches as to activate and embody a more robust and engaging theology of public life.

Cultivating Faith and Faithfulness in Public Life

How is public life transformed? How can communities of ANA Christians live out an exilic faith and faithfulness? These congregations have a unique opportunity to invest in and contribute to the character and beauty of public life. As Soong-Chan Rah challenges in his provocative book, *The Next Evangelicalism*, ANA congregations have a dynamic platform to speak into and influence the shape of the evangelical movement in the future.[13] But in addition, ANA churches can be pioneers and vanguards toward broader cultural renewal and transformation.

Developing an ANA Theology of Cultural Engagement

The church has pursued various approaches in relationship with its surrounding culture. In his classic work, *Christ and Culture*, H. Richard Niebuhr crafted an oft-critiqued paradigm of five historical dynamics or theological typologies.[14] At the two extremes, Niebuhr posits a Christian community that is antagonistic to its surrounding culture (Christ against culture) and one that is completely identified with it (Christ of culture). In between, there is a gnostic pattern (Christ above culture), a two-kingdom typology

(Christ and culture in paradox), and a missiological orientation (Christ transforming culture). Much of the way modern American Christians have viewed their identities and interactions in the public life has been derivative of Niebuhr's incisive analysis.

ANA Christians who seek to participate in public life ought to determine what their theology of cultural engagement is. Many ANA evangelicals have inherited the "Christ against culture" pattern. For them, the purpose of salvation is to be delivered from a fallen, sinful, and evil world. The goal of discipleship is purity in doctrine, holiness in lifestyle, and safety in a cloistered church community. Evangelism is limited to rescuing souls from divine judgment. Such a separatist theology of cultural engagement may not, in the long run, enable ANA believers to participate effectively in public life. Fortunately, Niebuhr offers other typologies that are more biblically grounded and offer much more satisfying rationale for public life.

Indeed, we believe that God is raising up a new generation of ANA Christians who desire a Christ-transforming-culture approach to their theology of cultural engagement. ANA Christians are no longer content to play a marginal role in God's mission to the world. Indeed, there are many significant opportunities to make a world of difference. But it begins with a clear idea of what type of Christ and culture typology ANA Christians bring to their discipleship. ANA Christians who wish to develop a theology of cultural engagement must be aware of one major limitation in Niebuhr's typologies. *Christ and Culture* assumes that culture is monolithic, when in fact there are many cultures and many publics. Infusing faith into all of life becomes very unclear when all of life is filled with complex multiplicities.[15]

The greatest temptation for ANA Christians is to assume that the mainstream is all that matters. While recognizing the real power differential between mainstream and margins, a better approach would be to appreciate how Christ is engaging in all cultures, not just the mainstream. Indeed, if ANA Christians only engage mainstream culture, our ethnic and racial distinctive will be lost in the conversation. That loss eviscerates our ability to participate in God's global activity in Asia and in race relations in North America.

We believe that ANA Christians have a missiological mandate to engage in all our cultures and publics. Because our contexts are ethnic (Chinese, Korean, Cambodian, etc.), racial (Asian Pacific North American), and mainstream, our theology of cultural engagement must necessarily be broad enough to encompass them all. By consciously engaging a multiplicity of contexts, ANA congregations can step forward in generative thinking and action. These churches can emerge as transformative communities that can model cultural renewal and public life integration. But how can we be transformative? Is it enough to issue forth ideas and opinions? Is it enough to evangelize and do acts of justice and mercy?

Making ANA Christian Culture

To assist in this journey, we turn to Andy Crouch's important perspectives in his book *Culture Making: Recovering Our Creative Calling*.[16] Crouch suggests that an appropriate posture to engage the different spheres of life is that of a gardener and of an artist. The former takes and stewards what has already been given to enhance and increase the beauty and good in life, while the latter possesses the capacity to see something new and create from that potential something substantive and beneficial. Both perspectives of cultivator and of creator are more helpful in transforming culture than simply proclaiming ideas that are true. Cultural artifacts that reflect a worldview, such as a song, a painting, a film, a community or organization, a building, or a life (vocation), can be much more transformative than simply persuading people of the veracity of certain beliefs. Such representations are especially helpful for forging a "public life praxis" for ANA Christians.

A core foundation in this process of culture creation and formation is the principle of vocation. Asian congregations in the North American context must discern and identify their unique voice in the *missio dei* (mission of God). These households are not merely to adopt the best practices of their evangelical neighbors, but should listen for and locate the distinctive flavor of their faith in public life. Indeed, our ANA history, experiences, identities, and cultures are the raw materials from which to create a unique voice (and representation) for public life. As has been already discussed in this chapter, the ANA church is emerging from a journey of self-exclusion and marginalization to find its future firmly grounded in the formative potential of cultural change and influence. What is most needed is to equip the church to articulate more clearly and affirm their God-given calling as communities pursuing faith and faithfulness in life through the process of culture making.

Strategies for ANA Christian Culture Making

This culture-making process involves three key dimensions. First, church leaders must be equipped to embrace and embody a theology of public life. Churches draw their visionary energy and courage from the passion and maturity of their leaders. Pastors and congregational leaders are critical people of influence. As such, the training and equipping of these men and women are vital for the broader public life formation throughout the church. This must take place both from the rigors of theological formation as well as through the praxis of public life and ministry. The skill set of future public life leaders will draw from the strengths and disciplines of the academy but also from the creative edge and energies of the workplace and society. Women and men who model and champion a pioneering spirit of public life will be grounded in a foundation of biblical theology as well as the innovation of the natural and social sciences, economics, business, and so on.

Second, the ANA church must also be equally committed to prepare and develop each person to engage faith in daily life. Much effort is necessary to remove the dichotomy between Sunday faith and Monday work. Too often spirituality is confined to religious activities and too rarely is woven into the fabric of daily living. ANA Christians can model faith-life integration in their workplaces, neighborhoods, and social communities. They can advocate and spearhead causes that advance biblical values of justice, reconciliation, and mercy. The One Day's Wage movement, initiated by Eugene Cho of Quest Church (Seattle), is an excellent example of the social justice entrepeneurship emerging from ANA churches. They can steward their intellectual and financial resources for the common good. They can share and advocate for those on the margins through partnerships with community organizations. Christians Supporting Community Organizing (www.cscoweb.org) and Christian Community Development Association (www.ccda.org) are valuable resources for such endeavors. Discerning, discovering, and unleashing the unique vocational calling of each person in the congregation is a vital capacity to be cultivated.

Finally, each congregation must capture its own missional voice and strengthen its commitment to a public life witness. To find a missional voice requires the hard work of self-discovery, something that is not readily available for ANA churches. Thus, intentional efforts to understand the history and culture of ANAs are necessary. In addition to understanding better the ANA context, ANA churches seriously need to consider their proximal context, which may have implications for the geographical location of its facilities or its members' places of residence. It highlights that the church is not to be separate from or outside of its community. Each congregation is a spiritual anchor in the community in which it resides. The church is not to be separate from or outside of its community. Rather than just being a matter of convenience or safety, the church recognizes its location to be a specific call to be the household of God.

Toward an Asian North American Theology and Practice of Public Life

Despite the difficult encounter with race and poverty, Pastor Tran, Anthuan and Sue Nguyen, and the rest of the congregation were undaunted. They decided to study their faith and ANA legacy more deeply. They discovered that Christ calls his people toward passionate engagement with public life. They realized that a better appreciation of the Vietnamese American story (and those of other marginalized people) could inspire their members to serve out of a deep understanding of their unique calling to help North American Christianity become more like the biblical vision of a global church.

The church leaders then started conversations with leaders from other churches in the neighborhood. As they built a multiracial co-alition of churches, they better understood the needs of the Vietnamese, the Asian American, and the wider communities. They discovered that they could partner with other faiths and community organizations around common public issues as well as global missions. Gradually, they learned how to engage public policy matters that really revitalized and transformed their community.

As their church became more aware of how it could participate in God's work in San Jose, they discovered resources for helping their members to relate to a world greater than their ethnic enclave. Sunday school resources were developed to help their members cultivate healthier families and more effective marketplace ministries. In the future, perhaps, they may attempt to become a multiracial congregation. But in the meantime, by pursuing a theology of public life, by building an ANA Christian culture, and by partnering with other churches and organizations, this church is on its way to becoming a positive public witness for the gospel.

✦
NOTES

1. Timothy Tseng, "Resident Aliens from a Different Shore: A History of Asian American Ministry through the Eyes of Asian American Christian Leaders," lecture presented at the inaugural conference of Seattle Pacific Seminary's Asian American Ministry Program, June 13, 2011. Rev. Takie Okumura (1865–1945) and Rev. Ng Poon Chew (1866–1931) were two prominent clergy leaders.

2. The rich legacy of pre-1965 ANA Christianity will soon be forgotten unless efforts are made to encourage historical research.

3. Barry A. Kosmin and Ariela Keysar, *American Religious Identification Survey (ARIS 2008)* (Hartford, CT: Trinity College ISSSC, 2009); The Pew Forum on Religion and Public Life, "U.S. Religious Landscape Survey, February 2008," http://religions.pewforum.org/pdf/report-religious-landscape-study-full.pdf (accessed November 15, 2011); Robert N. Bellah et al., *Habits of the Heart: Individualism and Commitment in American Life* (Berkeley: University of California Press, 1985). See also www.robertbellah.com.

4. Bellah, *Habits of the Heart.* See also www.robertbellah.com.

5. Robert B. Putnam, *Bowling Alone: The Collapse and Revival of American Community* (New York: Simon & Schuster, 2000).

6. The 80-20 Initiative is an example of a group advocating for Asian American racial equality in the political arena. See www.80-20initiative.net.

7. 80-20 Initiative. See http://www.80-20initiative.net.

8. Lisa Sun-Hee Park, *Consuming Citizenship: Children of Asian Immigrant Entrepreneurs* (Stanford, CA: Stanford University Press, 2005).

9. William R. Hutchison, *The Modernist Impulse in American Protestantism* (New York: Oxford University Press, 1976), and George M. Marsden, *Fundamentalism and American Culture: The Shaping of Twentieth-Century Evangelicalism, 1870–1925* (New York: Oxford University Press, 1980), are two classic studies.

10. See Margaret Lamberts Bendroth, *Fundamentalism and Gender, 1875 to the Present* (New Haven, CT: Yale University Press, 1996).

11. "A generation later, neo-evangelicals softened the bellicose tenor of their fundamentalist parents in efforts to reengage culture. But, for the most part, they inherited an outlook that compartmentalized faith from daily life." Joel A. Carpenter, *Revive Us Again: The Reawakening of American Fundamentalism* (New York: Oxford University Press, 1999).

12. See Charles Mathewes, *A Theology of Public Life* (Cambridge: Cambridge University Press, 2007). Mathewes distinguishes between a public theology and a theology of public life, arguing that the former fails to recognize the latter's interest in the ascetic process of spiritual formation of Christians as a critical element of discourse.

13. Soong-Chan Rah, *The Next Evangelicalism: Freeing the Church from Western Cultural Captivity* (Downers Grove, IL: InterVarsity, 2009).

14. H. Reinhold Niebuhr, *Christ and Culture* (San Francisco: Harper & Row, 1951).

15. We are aware of recent critiques of Niebuhr's Christ and culture typology, and one of them is precisely to say how it is no longer useful since the breakdown of monolithic culture in general and Christendom in particular. For more on critiques of Niebuhr's typology, see Stanley Hauerwas and William Willimon, *Resident Aliens* (Nashville: Abingdon, 1989), esp. 39–43; and Craig A. Carter, *Rethinking Christ and Culture* (Grand Rapids: Brazos, 2006).

16. Andy Crouch, *Culture Making: Recovering Our Creative Calling* (Downers Grove, IL: InterVarsity, 2008).

CHAPTER 9

✝

Extending Grace and Reconciliation

From Broken Households to the Ends of the Earth

JOHN E. CHUNG AND AL TIZON

Sandi walked out of the elders' meeting confused and frustrated. Having recently been accepted as a candidate by an urban mission organization called City Servants, she went into the meeting expecting affirmation, encouragement, and perhaps even a commitment to support her prayerfully and financially. What she encountered instead was a wall of questions, which exposed deep rifts regarding the nature of the church's identity and mission.

The elders, of course, did not intend to discourage Sandi, but some of them simply could not see the work she felt called to do as "missionary" in nature since it did not require going "overseas." Why did the nearby Hispanic neighborhood (where she planned to serve) need missionaries anyway, they asked in so many words. Sandi saw the irony of the church spending the majority of its annual mission budget on short-term mission trips to Mexico and Central America, while questioning the validity of ministering to the very same people in a nearby neighborhood, but she chose not to say anything.

Furthermore, in spite of her efforts to describe the holistic approach of City Servants—that is, its equal commitment to evangelism *and* social action—the elders peppered her with questions, such as, "What does justice have to do with missions?" and "When are you going to have time to evangelize?" The meeting grew tense as differences in vision got tangled up with personality clashes. She left the meeting thinking how "messed up" her church was and marveling at how the elders, despite claiming to have a strong passion for missions, seemed oblivious to the nature of the gospel as well as to current trends in mission.

Sandi had grown up in this church. Her parents, immigrants from Korea like most of the congregation, had been longtime members and lay leaders. Her father had even served as an elder at various points. However, for quite some time, Sandi had been feeling more and more alienated from her church, and this last elders' meeting only aggravated those feelings. She asked herself again with new intensity, "Do I even belong to this church anymore? I've always called it home, but the differences seem to be getting wider and wider." As she thought further and beyond her own personal frustration, she blurted out loud, "How can my church even think about missions when it has so many of its own issues to resolve?"

Too Broken to Do Mission?

This story reflects a range of experiences that many second- and third-generation Asian North American (ANA) Christians have experienced. Indeed, many of Sandi's generation share her sense of disconnect to the churches in which they grew up, particularly in the area of mission vision and strategy.

The question of the church's readiness "to change the world for Christ" in the face of its own conflicts, shortcomings, disagreements, and generational misunderstandings—in a word, its brokenness—is an important one and certainly not limited to ANA churches. How indeed can broken, dysfunctional households called local churches, themselves in desperate need of God's grace and reconciliation, possibly bear witness to the good news of Christ in the world?

As understandable as this question is, does it perhaps come from emotional impulse rather than clear thinking? The notion that churches must have their act together first before they engage the world in mission does not hold up under biblical scrutiny. The Bible attests to a God who intentionally chooses and uses broken imperfect people to accomplish God's purposes, as if broken vessels themselves carry with them the message of God's saving grace (2 Cor. 4:7; Rom. 7). In this light, it is our conviction that the very issues that local congregations deal with internally point the way for the church's mission in the world.

This conviction compels ANA churches first to look deeply and honestly at our own issues; and second, to consider these very issues not necessarily as impediments to mission, but ways to understand and practice mission itself. Again, this belief is applicable to all churches, for they are all broken in one way or another. But assuming that brokenness manifests itself differently from culture to culture, what are the internal issues that may be particular to ANA churches, and how can these in-house issues inform the way we engage the world in mission?

ANA Churches in Mission: An Assessment

The problem is certainly not that the ANA church is lagging behind in fulfilling the Great Commission (Matt. 28:18-20). In fact, if we include the missionary efforts of China, Korea, and the Philippines, a case can be made that Asian Christians take the lead in mission efforts today.[1] ANA churches can celebrate this alongside fellow Asians around the world. For example, the increasing number of ANA participants in InterVarsity's triennial Urbana Conference—from a mere handful in 1984 to making up just a little more than 30 percent of all participants in 2009—attests to the heightened desire and involvement of ANAs in both local and global outreach.[2] Yet, even as missions remains a key component in the ethos of ANA faith communities, insiders know all too well the internal issues that at first glance appear to be barriers to authentic mission.

These issues fall under two basic categories. The first is identity: what does it mean to be an ANA church? When a group identifies itself as ANA, it implies that it is no longer "purely" Japanese or

Vietnamese or Indian in cultural identity, but is transforming into a hybrid identity that has elements of both Asian and North American cultures. Who are we as ANA churches, and how does this "identity-in-progress" impact our relationship with and mission to other cultures? The second category is missiology: what is mission? And what are our approaches to mission? These basic questions draw out a range of complex issues that include globalization, holistic ministry, incarnational ministry, and postcolonialism. To these two questions we now turn.

Identity Issues

There are at least four cultural identity issues within the ANA church that inform mission in overtly significant ways: enculturation, ethnocentrism and racism, multiculturalism, and the quest for the American Dream.

Enculturation. The movement from immigrant status to enculturated status constitutes the first issue. To what extent do we expect an immigrant people to conform to North American culture? The process of enculturation—that is, the shift from a clear identity as a Cambodian or Taiwanese or Indonesian immigrant church to becoming Cambodian *American*, Taiwanese *American*, or Indonesian *American*—is inevitable. Enculturation—the process (formal and informal) of internalizing some of the lifeways of a culture in which one has been transplanted while also retaining some of the lifeways of one's original culture—is happening one way or another in ANA churches and indeed in all immigrant churches. Moreover, there are experiences that the various Asian ethnicities share among themselves that have warranted the pan-ethnic "Asian North American" designation, lumping these shared experiences and responses between specific Asian cultures into an integrated hybrid culture. To be an ANA, therefore, represents an identity-in-progress; or in the words of the late David Ng, ANAs are a "people on the way."[3]

Harking back to Sandi's experience, the mutual frustration she and the elders experienced stems from the dilemma of an identity-in-progress, of a church transitioning from being immigrant to becoming enculturated. Like all immigrant churches, Sandi's church began with the vision to serve a particular people group—in her case, Korean Christians who have moved to the United States, as well as to reach non-Christian Koreans with the gospel. The key word here is *Korean*. For many years, the church's reason-for-being has been its mission to its own specific people group. To many, especially those among the older members, the changes feel like a tragic loss of motherland identity, and therefore they resist. In contrast, the younger generation, enculturated through various venues of school, friends, and media, finds the older generation's posture of retaining the old and resisting the new difficult to understand.

Ethnocentrism and Racism. A second issue—ethnic preservation—takes the enculturation issue one level deeper. Naturally and understandably, first-generation ANAs tend to seek the preservation of the values and lifeways of their origins. The loss of cultural identity would be a travesty, not only for them but for future generations. We must not forget! For our children and grandchildren to disregard the traditions of the homeland is unacceptable. But to the second and third generations, such a posture amounts to ethnocentrism. In fact, some of the young interpret the tenacious grip of the first generation to the lifeways of the original culture as prejudicial, even racist—not necessarily intentionally, but ethnocentric nonetheless—as their parents and grandparents try extremely hard to retain the cultural "purity" of the church. One second-generation ANA church leader drives this sentiment home when he says, "Proof that we see as equal those whom we're serving in mission, is if we have no problem seeing our children marry them."[4]

Multiculturalism. A third interlocking issue of identity has to do with differing views of multiculturalism. Is being culturally homogenous valid in the context of a multicultural society, or should every church aspire toward becoming multicultural? ANA churches have approached this issue differently: Some work hard to retain elements of their Asian culture, which often results in a predominantly homogenous fellowship. Others work hard to diversify, while maintaining a primary focus on the ANA community. Others develop two services—one culturally specific, conducted in the mother tongue, and the other multicultural, conducted in English. Still others set out to be

intentionally multicultural. For example, City Line Church in Philadelphia was planted by Emmanuel Church, a large Korean American fellowship on the west side of the city. But church planter Steve
Kim was sent out not to plant another Korean American church, but
a congregation that reflects the cultural diversity of Philadelphia.[5]
Multiculturalism is an issue, and these churches have shown various
ways to deal with it.

One characteristic of a healthy ANA church, according to Helen
Lee, is that it "embraces the possibility of diversity" (Acts 15:8-11;
1 Cor. 12:13; Eph. 2:11-22).[6] It would be erroneous, therefore, to
interpret the famous Homogenous Unit Principle (HUP) as the end
of the story. HUP, the key component of church growth theory in the
1970s and '80s, basically refers to the idea that evangelism among
peoples of the same culture is more effective. In the words of HUP's
innovator Donald McGavran, people "like to become Christians
without crossing racial, linguistic or class barriers."[7]

HUP, however, does not have to result in permanently homo-
geneous churches. The Pasadena Statement, a document signed
by both champions and critics of HUP, still provides the definitive
word. It states: "All of us are agreed that in many situations a homogenous unit church can be a legitimate and authentic church.
Yet we are also all agreed that it can never be complete in itself."[8]
Indeed, as people grow in the gospel, which breaks down dividing
walls and calls all peoples to be one in Christ (Eph. 2:14), they become more open to the possibility of diversity.

The American Dream. A fourth identity issue is related to the
first three, but it does not fall as neatly between generations as the
others. We refer to the ANA quest for the American Dream, which
applies to all generations. Definitions abound for the term *American
Dream*, but it is essentially a commitment to a work ethic that promises prosperity, security, comfort, and self-actualization. Accurate or
not, suburbia as a lifestyle (or at least the stereotype of it) serves
as its symbol—a happy, stable family that lives in a big, detached
house faraway from danger with multiple rooms filled with all of
the comforts and "toys" the family desires. Convenience, comfort,

and luxury are all bought and maintained by a forty-, sixty-, or even eighty-hour workweek of one or both parents.

Asian immigrants have enculturated deeply into North American culture. The ANA stereotype of being the "model minority—a bright, shining example of hard work and patience whose example other minority groups should follow"[9]—refers precisely to how successful ANAs have been in fulfilling the Dream. As insulting as this stereotype is, like all stereotypes, there is an element of truth to it. "Asian [North] Americans' affluence and achievements," Ken Fong asserts, "have challenged the notion that to be a minority is to be disadvantaged."[10] Indeed, many ANAs have made good on the Dream, enjoying a very real level of success in the medical, scientific, business, and other white-collar sectors of society.[11]

While some ANA Christians take on the pursuit of the Dream as their own, others see it as diametrically opposed to the alternate dream of the kingdom of God and outright reject it. Fong quips, "Two Mercedes in the garage and three children at MIT are not what Jesus had in mind when he [talked] about the pearl of great price."[12] To the extent that ANA Christians live out the Dream, they must struggle, alongside millions of other North Americans, with the alluring power of materialism and consumerism. These two rival principalities have the potential to desensitize God's people to the plight of the lost and the poor, and therefore to God's mission in the world.[13] In this sense, the ANA church must be on guard against becoming *this* extensively North American, and to remember our primary allegiance to the kingdom of God.

Missiological Issues

The second basic set of issues in ANA churches that has direct bearing on outreach has to do with the understanding and task of mission itself—or in a word, *missiology*. Despite the remarkable rise of ANA mission scholars in the last twenty years,[14] there remains a lack of theological reflection on mission on the local church level. What is mission? And what are our approaches to mission? If we as

ANA churches revisit these two fundamental questions on a regular basis, our passion for mission—of which ANA churches have in abundance—would have the theological grounding that it needs. And if there was ever a time for the church universal to be theologically rooted, it is now, as the world experiences change so rapid and comprehensive that social philosophers and scientists can only call it "globalization."

Globalization is the "widening, deepening and speeding up of global interconnectedness, which has an all-encompassing impact upon the world."[15] As we look at this phenomenon through a missiological lens, the cultural ramifications of globalization necessarily come to the fore. We must consider the nature of mission and our approach to it in an age when

- technology has enabled the world to come to us;

- traditional mission fields have become mission-sending nations;

- "unreached people groups" are not limited within the boundaries of the so-called 10/40 Window (were they ever?), but living next door;[16] and

- the plight of the poor and oppressed also no longer fit neatly into geographical regions.

These issues highlight the multifaceted nature of mission in the twenty-first century, and ANA churches would do well to address them.

What Is Mission? Sandi and the elders butted heads at the meeting because they answered this question quite differently. While the elders operated on a traditional missionary paradigm that defines mission as the church sending missionaries "over there" to share the gospel with those who have not yet heard, Sandi operated on a new missional paradigm that defines mission as the church itself being sent *right where it is* to share the gospel with the church's neighbors in need. The locus of mission is the first obvious point of tension in answering the "What is mission?" question. Depending on where one stands on the immigrant-enculturation continuum determines how one understands mission. Those closer to the immigrant end (usually the older generation) see mission as sending specially called people, that is, missionaries, to faraway places. As such, the church participates in the Great Commission, but without changing the nature of the home church. Those closer to the enculturation end of the continuum (usually the second and third generations) see mission not so much as a "sending" body but as the church itself being sent by God right where it is located. With this mind-set, missional engagement begins with what the church does in its own backyard. Missionary activity within the surrounding neighborhoods will necessarily mean receiving non-Asians into the fellowship, and thus change the cultural constitution of the church.

In light of cultural globalization, wherein the nations have come together, Sandi is right to perceive mission as local. This is why the missional church movement has gained remarkable traction with the church in North America. Originally coined by Lesslie Newbigin in the UK and then popularized by the Gospel in Our Culture Network in North America, the term *missional* refers to the nature of the church as being sent by God to accomplish God's mission within its immediate locale.[17] The missional church paradigm refuses to view churches sending missionaries to faraway places as the complete picture; for if the church itself is sent, then it must engage its very context with the gospel. At the same time, the need for the gospel in many regions beyond North America's borders also urges the church not to lose sight of the-ends-of-the-earth nature of God's mission.

What is mission? Mission is bearing witness to the gospel message both locally and globally; to be Christ's witnesses "in Jerusalem, in Judea and Samaria"—that is, in our immediate communities as well as within our nation—"and to the ends of the earth"—crossing national borders and oceans (Acts 1:8). How the ANA church negotiates the relationship between the local and the global answers the first basic question in an important way.

Mission is also defined in how the ANA church negotiates word and deed in its understanding and practice of mission. While the elders at Sandi's church have continued to view evangelism as the primary (if not the sole) task of mission, Sandi has embraced a broader vision of mission that entails both evangelism and compassion and justice ministries. In light of the history of the evangelism versus social concern debate, it is easy to see why Sandi and the elders clashed at the meeting. The elders likely grew up in missionary-planted churches in Korea. As such, they inherited the conservative evangelical suspicion against anything even sounding like the liberal "social gospel," as well as the strong conviction that evangelism is the essence of mission.[18]

Sandi, on the other hand, grew up in a time when that debate had essentially run its course. And she is in good company, as the majority of evangelicals today have essentially adopted the view that the separation of the spiritual and the social is heretical, and that the task of mission is both proclamation and social engagement, that is, holistic. As Ronald J. Sider celebrates, "Almost all evangelical leaders now believe that evangelism and social ministry are both important parts of biblically shaped mission."[19]

What is mission? Mission is bearing witness to the gospel by both word and deed. The issue here is not choosing one understanding of mission over another so much as finding a way to engage in the holistic mission of the gospel together.

How Do We Approach Mission? The "how" question necessarily follows the "what" question. How does globalization shape the conversation around the church's approach to mission? Ironically, one of the repercussions of globalization has been the rise of a nationalist spirit among many peoples—an intense assertion of local cultural groups—that are forging postcolonial identities and thereby holding suspect anything that comes across as imperialistic. This would include certain missionary approaches. In light of a globalized world where postcolonial cultures are suspicious of any kind of condescending spirit, missionaries need to be acutely aware of the danger of operating under a colonial missionary paradigm, which basically assumed the sense of superiority that the colonizing culture possessed and proceeded to impose that culture's "superior" ways on native peoples as part of the church's evangelizing efforts.[20]

Some churches are more aware of this danger than others, as both colonial and postcolonial missionary postures can be detected in North American churches. Indeed, both well-meaning fundamentalists (who in their blind passion inadvertently impose their North

Americanized version of the gospel upon others) and nationalistic liberationists (who come off as anti–North American in their quest to present the gospel contextually) share the pews in many ANA churches. Most mission-informed Christians, however, probably fall somewhere in between, as they seek to bear witness to the gospel with cultural sensitivity.

ANA churches need to be aware of and deal with the varying responses to the colonial mentality in their missionary endeavors. Part of this awareness encompasses the different approaches of the church toward the world, that is, toward the lost, the poor, and the different. While some seek to maintain a safe distance from the world, serving the down-and-out but not in a way that necessarily changes us or our churches (what some call "the missionary compound mentality"), others among us have appropriated an incarnational approach, intentionally getting to know, living alongside, and befriending the underserved for the sake of the gospel, and thus undergo changes in ourselves.

The incarnational approach to mission has gained quite a following among the young adult population of the evangelical community, and many ANAs are counted among them. For example, New Hope Covenant Church is a multiethnic congregation located in a poor section of east Oakland in which 60 percent of its members are relocaters, that is, those who have been inspired by the incarnation of Jesus to live among the poor. Of the relocaters, 80 percent are ANAs.[21] The difference in approach to mission is, of course, not limited to the ANA church, but the gap between "safer" (more distant, at arm's length) and incarnational approaches among ANAs is exacerbated by the tensions of cultural identity already at play between the older and the younger generations.

These issues of identity and missiology, along with their respective sub-issues, get at the various tension points regarding mission that more or less run along generational lines in ANA churches. To be honest, "tension" says it kindly, for these issues represent deep rifts within ANA households of faith. Just ask Sandi or the elders and the generations they represent. For many second- and third-generation ANAs, these types of rifts are deep enough that they end up leaving the church of their youth in search of Christian communities that are more open to their understanding of mission. Some end up leaving the church completely. As for the first generation, many end up disillusioned themselves, feeling unappreciated ("If they only knew what we've been through to build this church"), disrespected ("They don't listen to us anymore"), and misunderstood ("They think we don't know what God's mission is"). Given all of these highly charged, internal issues, how can the ANA church even think about mission? How can it even think about transforming the world for Christ when the church itself is in desperate need of God's transformation?

A Biblical Pattern of Grace and Reconciliation

The saved-by-grace theology of God's household, which was established by Sydney Park in Chapter 1, provides a solid foundation on which to stand as we attempt to address this question. We are saved by grace and not by our own doing (Eph. 2:8). Beyond our brokenness, our need, and our inability to save ourselves, this theology emphasizes the merciful love of God extending salvation to those who do not deserve it (Rom. 3:10-26). But further, it also implies that we are not just *saved* by grace, we are also *sanctified* by grace, meaning that the perfecting of the body of Christ does not happen instantly; it happens rather through a process of grace-filled growth (John 14:25-26; 1 Cor. 3:1-17). In other words, when Christ saved us, God took on a project, a work in progress. Thus, from the first century until now, churches experience division and conflict within; for saved-by-grace members have not and will not come to full maturity until the end of time (Phil. 3:12-16).

But the truth that the church is a work in progress does not negate the responsibility to do good in the world. In fact, "We are what he has made us, created in Christ Jesus for good works, which God prepared beforehand to be our way of life" (Eph. 2:10, NRSV). The outpouring of grace through the cross demands an ethical response from the redeemed, broken as we still are. It demands, among other things, reconciliation between genders, races, socioeconomic classes, and generations in the body of Christ (Eph. 2:11-16; Gal. 3:28). It demands, as Park established, unity as the household's core nature. The working out of our salvation has much to do with learning to love one another across socially defined divides in order to be the holy temple of the Lord (Eph. 2:19-22) and to function as the one healthy body of Christ (Eph. 4:11-13).

The good news is that we do not have to wait until we are fully reconciled with one another before we share the gospel with others. In fact, we contend that the ways in which the church works out its salvation (by way of sanctification) should fundamentally inform the ways that the church engages the world in mission. As members of the church, we are saved by grace, and in the process of reconciliation with one another by the power of the gospel, we are simultaneously called to extend that grace and reconciliation to a lost and needy world. We are called to participate in God's mission despite the broken, imperfect state in which we know ourselves to be.

Extending grace and reconciliation to the world, even as we as household members work out our own salvation, defines God's mission in both purpose and method—God's purpose being the extension of grace and reconciliation to all, and God's method being the invitation to God's redeemed but still broken people to carry out this mission. Even a brief look at the formation and call of God's people—Israel in the Old Testament and the Jewish-Gentile church in the New—aptly demonstrates this biblical pattern.

The Formation and Call of Israel

It would have made more sense if salvation history began with God choosing the dominant nation of the times—great and glorious Egypt of old, for example—to carry out the divine mission throughout the world. But the biblical narrative reveals a different tack; Scripture describes God calling Abram, a member of the Hebrew people (Gen. 12:1-3; 17:4-5). Now, to be Hebrew in the ancient Near East was not exactly prestigious. On the contrary, it referred to "wandering peoples greatly restricted as regards financial means and without citizenship and social status."[22] And God chose them to stand tall among the nations. They would be great because first, it lifted up the name of the one true God, and second, it would demonstrate life under the rule of this God and thus reflect the benefits of citizenship in the kingdom of God for all to see.

The events surrounding the Exodus under the leadership of Moses gave birth to the nation of Israel. In Exodus 19:5-6, God covenanted with the newly liberated Hebrew slaves: "If you obey my voice and keep my covenant, you shall be my treasured possession out of all the peoples. . . . You shall be for me a priestly kingdom and a holy nation." To which the people replied, "Everything that the LORD has spoken we will do" (v. 8, NRSV). By doing so, the people of Yahweh accepted the stipulations of the covenant initiated by God essentially to become a contrast community that models the peace and justice that result from following the one true God. And as other people witness life under the rule of God, they draw near and hear the invitation to join the new community. This is the ultimate meaning of God's family (household) becoming a blessing to "all the families [households] of the earth" (Gen. 12:3, NRSV).

Those who would call this plan absurd have a point, for from a human standpoint, to be a blessing to the world is quite a tall order for a lowly group of desert nomads and former slaves! From a theological perspective, however, the plan reflects the absolute scandal of God's grace and power. And that is precisely the point: God called the unlikely, the needy, the barren, and the broken, and out of them God formed the nation of Israel—itself in desperate need of grace and reconciliation—to extend the same to all.

As loud and clear as Israel's failures come through in the pages of Scripture, God's faithfulness comes through louder and clearer. God did not renege on the covenant. "It is too light a thing that you should be my servant," said the Lord to his rebellious people in Isaiah 49:6, "to raise up the tribes of Jacob and to restore the survivors of Israel; I will give you as a light to the nations, that my salvation may reach to the end of the earth" (NRSV). Indeed, the biblical record reveals not only a God who chose the lowly of the world; it also shows a God who did not give up hope in Israel, despite her grave sins, to be the light of redemption in and for the world.

The Formation and Call of the Church

This pattern does not change as the story continues in the New Testament with the formation and call of the church. What *did* change was the shift from the hope of the kingdom to its fulfillment in the person of Jesus Christ. "The time is fulfilled," Jesus announced, "and the kingdom of God has come near; repent and believe in the good news" (Mark 1:15, NRSV). Jesus taught and preached the kingdom, and he lived out its righteousness, compassion, justice, and peace in his ministry (Luke 4:43; 7:22; Matt. 9:35).

Jesus embodied what the nation of Israel was called to be in the world (John 8:12); therefore, citizenship in the kingdom no longer hinged on Jewish heredity but on faith in Jesus Christ. This essentially paved the way for God's mission in the form of a new kind of community. The New Testament calls this new community the church, where grace abounds and where people—Jews and Gentiles, male and female, slave and free—enjoy righteousness, justice, peace, and reconciliation, because God reigns.

This call to be the church should sound familiar, since it simply continues the ancient call that was first heard by Abraham, developed in Moses, and taken on (albeit poorly) by the kingdoms of Israel and Judah; except now, the call is placed on a community of people whose central glue is faith in Jesus Christ. Empowered by the Holy Spirit, the church has taken on the ancient mantle to "bless all the families of the earth" and to "be light unto the nations." But just like God's people of old, the community called the church is made up of broken people in desperate need of God's grace and reconciliation themselves.

The very existence of the New Testament epistles demonstrates that the church was flawed from the beginning, for the letters were written and passed around to address issues, dilemmas, conflicts, and squabbles among the new followers of Jesus. But despite the problems that the new churches faced, the book of Acts shows that the *missio Dei* went forward in and through them. This is where God's *modus operandi* of choosing the lowly, the imperfect, and the broken to do God's will is seen most poignantly in the New Testament. In the same way that God acted in the past, God initiated a work—this time by sending the Son—with people who had no power to save or sanctify themselves and then called them to extend grace and reconciliation, which they themselves experienced, to the rest of the world.

Extending Grace and Reconciliation:
The Hope and Strategy

In light of the biblical evidence, we cannot understand the church without considering mission, and we cannot understand mission apart from the church. As Tite Tienou remarked at the opening of the consultation that inspired this book, "We must look at the church missiologically and mission ecclesiologically."[23] In this light, it is not too farfetched to claim, as we do here, that the body life of the church—warts and all—is not an obstacle to outreach, but a portal through which we can understand and practice God's mission in the world.

As ANA churches depend on grace and reconciliation in Christ, they engage the world in mission, extending that same grace and reconciliation to all. If ANA churches take this biblical understanding of church and mission seriously, several implications emerge that can serve as both the hope and the strategy for healthy missional ANA households of faith.

Humility in Mission[24]

The truth that we are saved and sanctified by grace requires a foundation of humility to undergird all of our missional activity. The late missiologist David J. Bosch called this the "vulnerability of mission."[25] Bosch distinguished between "exemplar missionaries" and "victim missionaries," the former being those who engage in mission as spiritual giants and heroic carriers of the gospel.[26]

Nathan Price, the missionary in Barbara Kingsolver's best-selling novel *Poisonwood Bible*, typifies this exempler missionary role.[27] Unbending and unteachable in his relationship with the native people, Price bungles the very message of the gospel by an easily correctible mispronunciation. Wanting to say, "Jesus is precious," he instead preaches for years, "Jesus is poisonwood." As an exemplar missionary, he not only embarrasses his family; he also alienates the very people he seeks to serve.

By contrast, "victim missionaries"—or those acutely aware of their own weaknesses and therefore of the absolute necessity of grace in their own lives—go about mission, in the famous analogy of evangelist D. T. Niles, like "a beggar telling another beggar where to find bread." They do not engage people of another culture presuming to have the answers; rather, they come with the openness to discover God and God's purposes along with the people. They do not come as soldiers on a crusade; rather, they come as guests showing gratitude and respect toward their hosts and an eagerness to interact with them.

The posture of a "victim missionary" counters the unfortunate historical association of evangelization with five hundred years of Western colonization. It also counters the colonial mentality that lingers in the international Christian missionary community today. ANA Christians find themselves in a peculiar place to demonstrate missional humility as historical victims of colonialism and/or marginalization. Their forbearers of the not-too-distant past were subject to colonial rule in both spheres of state and church. They have also experienced marginalization in a Eurocentric North America.[28]

This history, as well as the ongoing experience of being perpetual "strangers from a distant shore,"[29] should deter the ANA church from doing mission with an aura of superiority, and conversely prompt them to take on a posture of humility and service as they go about God's mission. Along with the passion that ANAs have demonstrated for cross-cultural mission, authentic humility—rooted not only in their own brokenness, but also in their experience of colonial missions and cultural marginalization—should undergird all that they do in the world for the sake of the gospel.

Intergenerational Outreach

While humility lays the foundation for biblical mission in the world, the next four missional implications come from specific issues with which many ANA churches struggle. The first of these has to do with the issue of the generations. How can the conflicts between first and second/third generations occurring in ANA churches—clashes in values, loyalties, ways of worship, and general misunderstandings—inform the practice of mission?

These clashes reverberate deeply enough that we view the "generation gap" not just in terms of age, but also in terms of culture. Indeed, the interaction between Asian immigrants resettling in America (first generation) and "Americanized Asian [North] Americans" (second and third generations)[30] is nothing less than a cross-cultural encounter, albeit within the same ethnicity. In terms of mission, this means at the very least that both new immigrants and the second and third generations caught between cultures need to be on the radar screen of ANA church mission. It is not an either/or proposition; ANA churches cannot forget to reach out to the immigrants who continue to come from the homeland as well as to reach out to the younger ANA generations. This implies a deep appreciation and respect for the lifeways of the homeland even as the church learns how to negotiate the North American cultural terrain.

Mission outreach is one area in which ANA churches can partner intergenerationally, as leaders foster understanding and missional partnership between the generations. Opportunities for growth and understanding are missed when adults, youth, and children do not work together in the forming and educating of a mission vision. The foci of ministry often differ between those who serve the immigrant first-generation and those who serve the English-speaking second and third generations, but mission outreach is one area where there can be equal footing.

Having a common vision for mission can truly strengthen a church. Binnerri Church, for example, is a Korean American congregation in Dallas that has successfully developed and practiced this common vision. When the church developed a mission focus in Yucatan, Mexico, they began sending volunteer teams to work with missionaries who serve a local church there. These teams are comprised of children from the family ministry, youth group members, the pastors, and members of both the Korean and English ministries.[31]

Another creative way that ANA churches can cultivate a deep appreciation and respect for their ethnicity, particularly for the second and third generations, is by forming and sending intergenerational mission teams to the motherland to partner with churches there. These kinds of trips provide the context for relationship building between the generations,[32] and provide the opportunity for the younger generation to experience firsthand the land of their parents and grandparents.

The sending out of missionaries is yet another area in which generations can partner. In the case of someone like Sandi, the first-generation congregation should take pride in seeing their own children wanting to serve as missionaries and desire to support her. Her peers should also see that she is one of their own and take part in supporting her as a missionary. How beautiful it would be to offer intergenerational support to those whom the church sends out.

Multiethnic Outreach

A third implication for mission in light of the biblical pattern of grace and reconciliation is that the church's outreach must extend beyond ANAs. If intergenerational outreach calls ANA churches to serve their own in every generation, then multiethnic outreach calls them to grasp the culturally universal scope of the gospel. A very common struggle in many ANA churches falls along the lines of "Should it remain intentionally ANA, or does every church need to strive to be multiethnic in order to be faithful to the gospel?" We believe the answer is yes and yes.

Insofar as a church seeks to be a gospel church, it will proclaim the power that has broken down the dividing walls of gender, race, and class (Gal. 3:28; Eph. 2:14), but it will also appreciate, affirm, and celebrate its ethnic identity. As Melba Maggay observes: "Cultures have an enduring integrity that we do well to guard and keep against forces that would seek to make us all the same. Diversity, not homogeneity, is God's design for the world. Let us remember this whenever we are face to face with pressures to surrender our rootedness and peculiarities as a people in the name of that faceless, often tasteless process called globalization."[33]

Indeed, to reach out multiethnically does not require losing one's specific ethnic identity. On the contrary, true cultural diversity depends on people who value who they are ethnically, for true diversity is a mosaic not a melting pot. True diversity calls for ANAs to *be* ANA, appreciating, affirming, and celebrating one's ethnicity. Only when ANAs are secure in themselves can they become open to a truly multiethnic church experience. Such a posture can manifest in ANA churches primarily serving ANAs, while expanding their mission vision to include all peoples. The picture toward which ANA churches should work is to maintain its ANA culture while not losing sight of "the eschatological call for the church to become a preview of coming attractions; for there is still coming a time when persons from every nation, tribe, people, and language will be gathered around the throne of the Lamb to worship him."[34]

Missionally speaking, this means a commitment to preaching the gospel to *all* peoples, beginning with our own. It means taking full advantage of what Andrew Walls calls "the Ephesian Moment," which refers to a time when the cultures of the world have come together in an unprecedented way.[35] In light of globalization, the possibilities for reaching across cultures are found in our own communities and neighborhoods.

As ANA churches do mission among a diversity of people in their own backyards and the fruit of their labor begin to join them for worship, the makeup of these churches can and does become more colorful in time. "Our initial focus was to reach second- and third-generation Asian [North] Americans and their friends," remembers Steve Wong, pastor of an ANA church in the San Francisco Bay Area. "Once we started realizing that vision, I saw that 'and their friends' meant becoming more multiethnic."[36]

The Antioch church in the book of Acts is a prime example of how Christians across cultures can come together to plant new multicultural churches. Acts 11:20 tells us that "men from Cyprus and Cyrene, went to Antioch and began to speak to Greeks also, telling them the good news about the Lord Jesus" (NIV). Up to this point the gospel was being preached primarily to those of Jewish background, but in Antioch God called Jews and Gentiles to form an intentionally multiethnic church. By contrast, too many English ministries of ANA congregations break off the mother church out of frustration and start multiethnic fellowships. This is often a painful process that results in anger and resentment on both sides. Perhaps if ANA churches today are as intentional as the Antioch church plant, the resentment of painful breaks can be replaced by the celebration of giving birth to multiethnic churches.

The "Antioch model" is exemplified by two churches in Boston—the Korean Church of Boston (KCB) and Primera Iglesia. KCB had for years fostered a ministry partnership with a church in Nicaragua. One year they realized that the annual volunteer short-term team would be greatly enhanced if it included Spanish speakers. So KCB asked Primera Iglesia, a Hispanic sister church within the same denomination, if it would like to join them in the mission to Nicaragua. Primera Iglesia agreed, and the churches began to partner together in sending out a joint team to Nicaragua every year. This relationship has continued to foster a deeper relationship between the two churches and more effective cross-cultural mission as the two congregations have begun sharing their respective gifts, resources, and language abilities with each other.[37]

Local and Global Outreach

Another issue within ANA churches that can inform a church's mission theology and practice is the geographical scope of mission. While for some the very word *missions* already carries with it a faraway global connotation, for others it has come to convey more of an outlook that begins locally, where the lost and the poor also reside. In light of the biblical nature of mission, seen most poignantly in the Great Commission (see Acts 1:8), the church's outreach must be local, global, and everywhere in between.

The "local versus global" debate with regard to the church's mission is ultimately a misguided one.[38] Mission does not refer primarily to *where*, but to *what* the church is doing for the sake of the gospel. What if churches came to regard gospel work as genuine mission whether it occurs a thousand miles away across the ocean or just a few blocks away across the street? To hark back to the exchange between Sandi and the elders, the mission she proposed in a nearby Hispanic neighborhood is as legitimate a work of mission as the trips that the church takes to Latin American countries every year. How can ANA churches think more strategically about their mission focus to include both local and global efforts?

One avenue through which this local-global (glocal?) understanding can be put into practice is the ever-popular short-term missions. Regardless of how one views short-term mission, the practice is on a remarkable rise in terms of the number of Christians taking part in them.[39] As such, why not guide ANA churches to include long-term partnership and follow-up in their practice of short-term missions?

Another strategy would be to send short-term mission teams locally as well as globally, for there are needs within North America as well as around the world. A local mission trip, for example, can be organized to go to an area in the country struck by disaster. A ministry team can also be formed to serve the international community in the church's backyard. About 700,000 international students and their families come to North America every year from traditionally mission-receiving countries.[40] The United States also receives up to 80,000 refugees each year from some of the most vulnerable places in the world.[41] This includes as many as 35,500 people from Near and Southeast Asia, and another 19,000 from East Asia.[42] These add to the steady flow of other immigrants to North America, a flow that increases the ethnic populations in both urban and suburban communities.

Of course, there are also many global possibilities for short-term teams to join in supporting the efforts of long-term missionary partners whom the church has been supporting financially and through prayer. Sharing the church's mission resources (both financial and human) between local and global efforts on a regular basis will surely help to render the local versus global debate obsolete in the ANA church.

Holistic Outreach

A final implication of the Bible's pattern of mission for ANA churches has to do with the balance of evangelism and social justice ministries. Few churches escaped the battle that raged for the soul of mission during the greater part of the twentieth century. Is the essence of mission soul-winning (evangelism), or is it the betterment of society and justice? At one point in the historical controversy, Bosch asserted that "the position that one could have both evangelism and social action became virtually untenable."[43]

The wholeness of the gospel, of course, challenges this either/or thinking, for the gospel has both personal and social dimensions. Authentic biblical mission cannot pit word against deed or vice versa. From a kingdom perspective, "evangelization without liberation, a change of heart without a change of structures, vertical reconciliation (between God and people) without horizontal reconciliation (between people and people), and church planting without community building" reflect missional shortsightedness.[44] Reminding each other of just how comprehensive the gospel is provides the first indispensable step in developing a truly holistic theology and practice of mission.

On a local church level, in addition to teaching, preaching, and practicing both evangelism and social justice, how can the church commit to supporting other local and global ministries that are holistic? What if holism became the criterion to help determine whether the church will financially support or partner with a ministry? For example, second only to the importance of relationships, the "Criteria for Support" document of City Line Church, an ANA congregation in Philadelphia, states, "CLC supports missionaries and/or ministries that are committed both to evangelism (verbal proclamation) and social concern (visible demonstration). We prefer supporting those who approach people and communities in word and deed over those who just do word or deed."[45]

Mission Marches On

From broken households to the ends of the earth, the *missio Dei* marches on, extending grace and reconciliation to all in and through a people in progress. This is what the biblical pattern reveals regarding mission: a God who has chosen a broken and imperfect people in order to reach all peoples. To allow our brokenness to impede our participation in the *missio Dei* would be a travesty. We are convinced that the very issues with which ANA churches struggle are windows through which we can peer to understand our mission in the world:

- The humility needed to learn from one another in the cultural and generational amalgam of the ANA church is the very humility that should wrap all of our missionary endeavors in the world.

- The work needed for the first and second/third generations to understand one another reminds us that we must address the needs of both immigrant and enculturated populations within our own people group.

- The tension between homogeneity and multiculturalism points to an approach to mission that at once celebrates our cultural identity and strives to reflect the diversity of the gospel.

- The tension between local and global mission points to an approach to mission that sees the need of the gospel on both local and global levels.

- And finally, the tension between evangelism and social justice points to the need to proclaim the gospel by both word and deed.

Imagine with us a continuation of the story of Sandi and the elders in light of this understanding of God's mission. What Sandi wanted to hear from the elders was, "Sandi, we are so excited that you want to be a missionary. How can we help?" Despite her disappointed expectations, she fights off the temptation to leave the church. Asking God for humility and patience, she is determined to pursue the mission to which she feels called while continuing to work humbly and respectfully with the elders of her church.

The elders also reflect on the meeting with Sandi and feel badly about how things ended. After a special meeting of the elders, they invite Sandi to the next official meeting to discuss further her mission plans. They really want to know more about her understanding of mission, and in turn, the elders would also like to tell her their understanding of mission. At that next meeting, the elders will ask questions, such as:

- What does it mean for you to be Korean American?

- We heard your passion for mercy and justice, which we affirm, but what is your understanding of evangelism?

- Is it possible for us to get involved in the community you'll be serving? If so, how?

- Would you also be willing to come to El Salvador with us?

Whether they will ever come to full agreement on these and other questions concerning mission, the elders feel a sense of pride that one of their young people is choosing a life of mission. They desire to support Sandi as much as possible. They are not naïve to think, however, that issues, questions, and conflicts concerning the mission of the church will not arise between the older and younger generations; the church is still a work in progress—at times, even a mess. But in light of the Scriptures, they also know that they must nonetheless live out the call to extend the grace and reconciliation of Christ to the world, and they must strive to do it together.

✦

NOTES

1. See, e.g., the various chapters in Timothy Park, ed., *Asian Mission: Yesterday, Today and Tomorrow* (Pasadena: Institute for Asian Mission, 2008).

2. Christy Chappell, e-mail correspondence to authors (December 18, 2009). Chappell served as the communications director for Urbana '09.

3. David Ng, ed., *People on the Way: Asian North Americans Discovering Christ, Culture, and Community* (Valley Forge, PA: Judson, 1996), xvii–xix.

4. Participant in the Global Mission Track of the ANA Consultation on Theology and Ministry, Trinity Evangelical Divinity School, Deerfield, IL, May 19, 2009.

5. For more information on City Line Church, go to www.citylinechurch .net/.

6. Helen Lee, "Hospitable Households," in *Growing Healthy Asian American Churches*, eds. Peter Cha, Steve Kang, and Helen Lee (Downers Grove, IL: InterVarsity, 2006), 141–42.

7. Donald McGavran, cited in "The Pasadena Statement," in *Making Christ Known*, ed. John Stott (Grand Rapids: Eerdmans, 1996), 62.

8. Lausanne Committee for World Evangelism, "The Pasadena Statement," in *Making Christ Known*, ed. John Stott (Grand Rapids: Eerdmans, 1996), 64.

9. C. N. Le, "The Model Minority Image," Asian Nation website, www. asian-nation.org/model-minority.shtml#ixzz0T1RIJtNT (accessed November 15, 2011).

10. Ken Uyeda Fong, *Pursuing the Pearl: A Comprehensive Resource for Multi-Asian Ministry* (Valley Forge, PA: Judson, 1999), 15.

11. Ronald Takaki, *Strangers from a Distant Shore: A History of Asian Americans*, rev. ed. (Boston, MA: Little, Brown, 1998). Renowned historian Ronald Takaki establishes that while many ANAs have "made it," there are others who have most certainly not made it, many earning low wages, living in impoverished conditions, and experiencing the social marginalization along with the other minorities in the country. See esp. pp. 474–84. This sobering truth should prevent anyone from taking the "model minority" stereotype too seriously.

12. Fong, *Pursuing the Pearl*, 16.

13. See Soong-Chan Rah, *The Next Evangelicalism: Freeing the Church from Western Cultural Captivity* (Downers Grove, IL: InterVarsity, 2009), 46–63, where the author takes a sobering look at the grip of consumerism and materialism on North American society.

14. For example, a cursory review of the Dissertation Notices in the *International Bulletin of Missionary Research* for 2008–9 yields 38 out of 113 (a quarter of the total) completed by Asian or Asian American mission scholars.

15. David Held, Anthony McGrew, David Goldblatt, and Jonathan Perrtaon, cited in Al Tizon, *Transformation after Lausanne* (Eugene, OR: Wipf & Stock, 2008), 86.

16. Abundant information about ethnic people groups is available today. According to the Joshua Project, a ministry of the U.S. Center for World Mission and the Center for the Study of Global Christianity at Gordon Conwell Theological Seminary, there are an estimated 15,900 people groups in the world. Among these numbers around 6,700 of them are considered unreached or least reached, meaning they have little or no exposure to the good news of Jesus Christ. Despite the 10/40 Window campaign to try to channel missionaries to these parts, 85 percent of the missionary force is still concentrated in places where national churches already exist. To learn more about the Joshua Project, go to www.joshuaproject.net.

17. There is a fast-growing bibliography of books on the missional church, but to grasp the original intent of those responsible in popularizing it in the North America, see Darrel Guder, ed., *The Missional Church: The Sending of the Church in North America* (Grand Rapids: Eerdmans, 1998).

18. For a more detailed account of the history of the evangelism versus social concern debate among missionaries, see Tizon, *Transformation after Lausanne*, 21–36.

19. Ronald J. Sider, cited in Tizon, *Transformation after Lausanne*, xiii.

20. For more detailed treatment of this connection, see F. Albert Tizon, "Remembering the Missionary Moratorium: Toward a Missiology of Social Transformation in a Postcolonial Context," *Covenant Quarterly* 62, no. 1 (February 2004): 13–34.

21. To learn more about New Hope Covenant Church, go to www .newhopeoakland.org.

22. Burton Goddard, "Hebrew, Hebrews," in *New International Dictionary of the Bible*, ed. J. D. Douglas and Merrill C. Tenney (Grand Rapids: Zondervan, 1987), 425.

23. Tite Tienou, opening remarks for the Asian North American Consultation on Theology and Ministry, Trinity Evangelical Divinity School, Deerfield, IL (May 18, 2009).

24. This section relies heavily on, and in some cases simply lifts sentences from Tizon, "Remembering the Missionary Moratorium," 17–18.

25. David J. Bosch, "The Vulnerability of Mission," in *New Directions in Mission and Evangelization 2*, eds. James A. Scherer and Stephen B. Bevans (Maryknoll, NY: Orbis, 1999), 73.

26. Ibid., 80–83.

27. Barbara Kingsolver, *Poisonwood Bible* (New York: HarperCollins, 1998).

28. For a personal reflection on this type of marginalization from an ANA perspective, see Al Tizon, "I Am Asian, Hear Me Roar!" *Prism* 16, no. 5 (September–October 2009): 7. The reflections in this article are in response to reading Rah's *The Next Evangelicalism*.

29. This description of Asian Americans is the chosen title of Takaki's book on a history of Asian Americans: *Strangers from a Distant Shore*.

30. Fong, *Pursuing the Pearl*, 8–14.

31. These were mission trips to the Yucatan Mexico between 1997 and 2000. See www.binnerri.org.

32. Peter Cha, Paul Kim, and Dihan Lee, "Multigenerational Households," in *Growing Healthy Asian American Churches*, ed. Peter Cha, S. Steve Kang, and Helen Lee (Downers Grove, IL: InterVarsity, 2006), 157–59.

33. Melba P. Maggay, *Jew to the Jew, Greek to the Greek: Reflections on Culture and Globalization* (Quezon City, Philippines: Institute for Studies in Asian Church and Culture, 2001), 56.

34. Fong, *Pursuing the Pearl*, 7.

35. Andrew Walls, *The Cross-Cultural Process in Christian History* (Maryknoll, NY: Orbis, 2002), 78–81.

36. Lee, "Hospitable Households," 141–42.

37. This partnership began in 2005. See www.kcboston.org and www.presbyteryofboston.org/Primera_Iglesia.

38. Until the emergence of the missional church movement, mission courses in most seminaries have had to do with gospel work in other lands, while evangelism and ecclesiology courses have dealt with the domestic situation. This has not been remedied by a long shot, but more and more mission and evangelism scholars have detected the discrepancy and are poised to correct it. For example, the architects of the formal missional church movement in the United States, such as Darrel Guder, Lois Barrett, Craig Van Gelder, George Hunsberger, and others, have made their way into the American Society of Missiology (ASM), an academy historically dominated by conventional missionaries and practical Christian anthropologists. Furthermore, the Academy for Evangelism in Theological Education (AETE) recently attached itself to ASM, holding its annual meeting at the same time and in the same location as ASM so that mission and evangelism, and global and local mission, can be seen, discussed, and studied together. These convergences in the academy reflect a positive shift in thinking regarding the spatial scope of mission.

39. For a recent study on short-term missions, see Robert J. Priest and Joseph Paul Priest, "They see everything, and understand nothing," *Missiology* 36, no. 1 (January 2008): 53–73.

40. Institute of International Education (2010), "International Student Enrollment Trends, 1949/50–2009/10," Open Doors Report on International Educational Exchange, www.iie.org/opendoors (accessed September 30, 2011).

41. According to the USA Immigration and Nationality Act, the ceiling for refugees entering the United States in 2008 was 80,000; this figure was renewed in 2011.

42. Statistics from U.S. Department of State, Proposed Refugee Admissions for FY 2010—Report to Congress, cited in Daniel C. Martin, "Annual Flow Report: Refugees and Asylees 2010" (DHS Office of Immigration Statistics, May 2011), 2, www.dhs.gov/xlibrary/assets/statistics/publications/ois_rfa_fr_2010.pdf (accessed September 30, 2011).

43. David J. Bosch, "In Search of New Evangelical Understanding," in *Word and Deed: Evangelism and Social Responsibility*, ed. Bruce J. Nichols (Grand Rapids: Eerdmans, 1986), 71.

44. Tizon, *Transformation after Lausanne*, 6.

45. Mission Team of City Line Church, "Criteria for Support" (unpublished document written by Mission Team of City Line Church, Philadelphia, October 2007).

CONCLUSION

✝

Moving Forward and Outward

SOONG-CHAN RAH

This collection of essays reflects the culmination of an effort to form an ecclesiology relevant for the Asian North American (ANA) church. Our hope for the ongoing formation of ANA ecclesiology is that it would bless—encourage, enrich, grow, equip, and challenge—not only the ANA church, but the whole church of Jesus Christ in all of its rich diversity. The book represents our attempt to integrate various experiences and perspectives from the ANA community in order to move toward a healthy and robust ecclesiology. We believe that the intersection of the scholarly disciplines of theology (the academy) with the practices of the church (pastoral reality) has the potential to generate a theology that serves the whole church.

At times the church may hold a pessimistic view on the state of academic theology and the relevance of theological education. Academic theology may be perceived as an ivory tower exercise that generates competition between different disciplines within theological education. As theologian Edward Farley claims, "[It is] almost impossible for the scholarly-guild mind-set to think about theological education in any other way except through the self-evident categories of the guild discipline."[1] On the other hand, theological educators may become frustrated with the overly pragmatic approach often appropriated by the local church.

A robust ecclesiology provides the necessary bridge between biblical theological concepts and on-the-ground practices of the church. The hope in convening the range of academics and practitioners, in both the consultation and this book, was to contribute to the building of this bridge, as we engaged as a community of ANA scholar-practitioners. On one level, ecclesiology provides a description of the church, both in its present form and in its historical and traditional form. On a more fundamental level, ecclesiology serves the church by offering relevant biblical-theological reflections in which practical ministry realities can be firmly grounded. While we can assume that theology is a gift received from God, it is a gift from God that provides a benefit for God's people. As Ellen Charry states, "The great theologians of the past . . . were striving to articulate their pastoral value or salutary—how they are good for us. . . . When Christian doctrines assert the truth about God, the world, and ourselves, it is a truth that seeks to influence us."[2] Our best hope for this work is that the church in general and the ANA church in particular embody Christ's intentions not only for the household of the redeemed, but for the whole household of humanity.

The ANA Context and Ecclesiology

The specific location of the ANA community has to be considered when formulating a relevant ecclesiology. Because this project emerges out of the ANA context, there was a presupposition that the emerging theological and pastoral findings would reflect that social context. The initial consultation that sparked this work did not occur in a social vacuum. The individual participants arrived with a set of experiences that represented the ANA community. At the same time, the plenary sessions, individual interactions, and processing as a gathered community led to the formation of an ecclesiology that moves beyond the immediate social context of the individual participants. The sense of a common calling and purpose coupled with the understanding of the particularities of the ANA community results in a theological inquiry that attempts to derive a sense of direction and a trajectory specific to the ANA community but with application for the entire church. As specific issues were being addressed, a unique expression of ecclesiology emerged that challenges the entire Christian community to express itself fully as the household of God. Understanding the social context of the ANA community, therefore, was a key step forward toward a robust ecclesiology. Our hope is that the practices of the church that emerge out of the unique context of the ANA community contribute to the larger understanding of ecclesiology.

A robust ecclesiology that applies to the broader context of North American Christianity is hopefully one of the products of this work. Several factors contribute to the formation of the ANA church and lead to an application that expands beyond the specific context to the broader church. Three of the key factors include the role of community in forming ecclesiology, consideration of the specific influence of the social context of North American evangelicalism, and the complexity of addressing generational issues.

Doing Ecclesiology in Community

The first critical practice is the formation and embodiment of community. It is in Christian community where we learn "to interpret, and to have our lives interrogated by, the scriptural texts such that we are formed and transformed in the moral judgment necessary for us to live faithfully before God."[3] The consultation community worked together to learn from one another and to move toward a relevant ecclesiology. The project sought to encompass the range of different perspectives and experiences within the ANA community. These priorities reflect important practices applicable to the ANA church and to the larger context of Christian theology.

The process of growing and developing as a community of scholar-practitioners was as, if not more, important than the end product of this book. Indeed, the demonstration and embodiment of the spiritual practice of reflection on Scripture and community life may prove to be the most significant contribution. The practice of listening to a range of voices proved to be an important one, coupled with the practice of searching the Scriptures as a community. Given the highly communal nature of the ANA social context, could one of the unique aspects of ANA ecclesiology be the formation of biblical and pastoral theology through the context of community? The increasing diversity of North American Christianity at large requires the formation of a broader and deeper community for theological engagement that speaks to this reality.

Even within the ANA community, the ongoing challenge is to engage the voices that are often excluded. The overwhelming population of this gathering was well-educated, middle-class, East Asian evangelicals. The trajectory of the ANA community requires engaging with more women in leadership, the South and Southeast Asian communities, as well as an attempt at geographic diversity. Practical theology arises out of a particular context. In order to express a legitimate theological enterprise, future efforts should include the breadth of the ANA community in that context. In the same way, North American ecclesiology should relate and reflect the diversity of contexts that now comprise North American Christianity.

Negotiating Asian and North American Christian Contexts

A second important practice in the formation of ANA ecclesiology also relates to the connection between specific context and broader ecclesial development. A significant portion of ANA ministry is formed in the context of North American evangelicalism. Many ANA pastors are graduates of evangelical seminaries and involved with evangelical denominations and networks. ANA ecclesiology and practical theology should arise from biblical foundations as a reflection of the evangelical nature of the majority of ANA churches.

At the same time that we participate in broad evangelicalism, most ANAs also maintain an outsider status in North American Christianity. As "the model minority," the ANA community is seen as representing the triumph of North American expressions of Christianity as they exemplify the successful hegemonic power of North American evangelicalism. Simultaneously, many ANA Christians still hold their home culture in high esteem and understand that their identity as foreign-born or second-generation immigrant may mean that they will not ever attain full acceptance in North American society.

This reality of being simultaneously an insider and an outsider dictates the experience of liminality (an in-between stage) often characteristic of the ANA community. This unique intersection of a highly Westernized form of Christianity (North American evangelicalism) with a bicultural worldview arising out of the liminal experiences of the ANA community, forms the ethos for the ANA Christian community. How such a community responds to this unique formation is key to the formation of an ecclesiology and practical theology for the ANA Christian community.

Negotiating the Generations

Finally, in addition to the influence of the evangelical ethos, this work also reflects the absolute importance of generational issues for both the ANA church and for the broader North American Christian community. The larger Christian community is experiencing the shift from an ecclesial framework built for baby boomers to one that is post–baby boomer. The shift from modernity to postmodernity, colonial to postcolonial, and Christendom to post-Christendom all underlie the generational shift in American Christianity. Generational shifts in American Christianity are not necessarily a new phenomenon; however, the added complexity of a generational shift in a growing immigrant community with the depth of change in American society deepens the need to grasp emerging generational dynamics.

The ANA church is also undergoing a generational shift and experiencing the *anomie* and liminality of this shift. The next generation of believers in the ANA church stands at the frontline of the complex issue of generational transitions. The lessons drawn from this generational shift in the ANA context should serve all elements of North American Christianity experiencing a similar type of shift. While the generational dynamics differ in many ways between different people groups and communities, the common experience of generational transitions should provide a context of rich learning from the diverse communities that now comprise North American Christianity.

Final Reflections

The Catalyst consultation, from which this book has sprung, was an attempt to embody the practice of forming community around the Scriptures in order to form a relevant ecclesiology for the unique context of the ANA church. The specific experience of the ANA community also relates to the larger move of God in the North American context. The range of issues that shape ANA ecclesiology provides a specific example that speaks to the broader context.

The positive impact of this project arises from the process of ecclesial formation, the attempt to form a beneficial theology, as well as the potential for application to the broader North American church. This project would not have been possible without the formation of a community that reflected together on Scripture and sought to develop an ecclesiology that serves both the ANA church and the North America church. The book would have little meaning without the process and the actual embodiment of the practices that undergird the work. This ecclesiology, therefore, owes a deep gratitude to all of the participants and the churches they represent.

✦
NOTES

1. Edward Farley, *Theologia: The Fragmentation and Unity of Theological Education* (Eugene, OR: Wipf and Stock, 1994), 15.

2. Ellen Charry, *By the Renewing of Your Minds: The Pastoral Function of Christian Doctrine*, Kindle ed. (New York: Oxford University Press, 1997), 17–45.

3. Stephen Fowl and L. Gregory Jones, *Reading in Communion: Scripture and Ethics in Christian Life* (Eugene, OR: Wipf and Stock, 1998), 34.

AFTERWORD

✝

BIAK MANG

This book offers a hopeful model of the Christian church for Asian North American congregations. Using the biblical metaphor of the church as the household of God, the editors recognize that faithful Asian North American Christians, including those from Burma, are still learning the true meaning of the church.

Honoring the Generations offers stories, theology, and concepts that are practical and applicable for Burmese* Christians, who are relative newcomers in North America. Like most immigrant groups, we struggle over issues of nurturing multigenerational leadership, maintaining our cultural values, negotiating gender issues, and navigating our complex relations to Burma, which are still oriented along distinct ethnic lines.

Burmese churches in North America are of two different types. The first is comprised of well established churches founded by early immigrants that offer worship services in English as well as in their native language. This book will help the first generation to understand the second and third generations in many ways. It will also help the younger generation to honor and appreciate the older generation.

The second type of Burmese church in North America is the immigrant congregation, peopled with recent arrivals from Burma or the refugee camps in neighboring nations. For newly arrived immigrants, the congregation is the center of the community, a "social oasis" as Sydney Park says. There they participate in worship, yes, but they also share community issues, interpret political and social information, and discuss other business. These congregations will often have few programs for youth or children—in part because the younger generation has less interest in participating in church activities rooted in preserving the culture of a homeland they may have never seen. This volume challenges newly established Burmese immigrant churches to recognize that our new setting will require new responses.

Because all members are equal in the household of God, the Burmese churches must pursue ministries attentive to our new challenges. For example, we must pay particular attention to youth and children ministry. We should allow our children and youth to question, to doubt, and to experiment among us, even though this approach contrasts with traditional culture in Burma. Many Burmese Christian parents consign the spiritual welfare of their children to the church, but this book reminds us of the importance of spiritual mentoring, discipleship, and daily Christian practice at home. Although the traditional Burmese family is hierarchical, this book encourages us to live into biblical patterns of right relationship between husband and wives and parents and children in the Christian family. While Burmese churches in North America exist for the spiritual well-being of their members and to support their former congregations back in Burma, this book challenges us to broaden our horizons to include mission work beyond our people, to encompass interfaith relationships and good citizenship.

This book reminds us that God's grace should not be misused. Our experiences in the Burmese diaspora should help form our identity as faithful Christians. This book challenges us to remember that no matter our ethnic, tribal, or theological background, we all are members of the household of God. Thus, we need to seek reconciliation, unity, and peace with one another, and that Christians from Burma should be encouraged to engage in relationships with other ethnic and racial groups. Every Asian North American pastor and church leader should read this book to understand the specific challenges of our congregations, and the general call to us all to pursue a fuller portion of God's grace for our people as part of the whole people of God.

* Technically, *Burmese* refers to the majority people group of Burma. While the vast majority of refugees from Burma are from other ethnic groups (e.g., Chin, Kachin, Karin), in this context it is simplest to use the term *Burmese* to refer to all immigrants from Burma.

ABOUT THE
CONTRIBUTORS
✝

Peter T. Cha is associate professor of pastoral theology at Trinity Evangelical Divinity School in Deerfield, Illinois. He is 1.5-generation Korean American.

John E. Chung is minister of missions at Park Street Church in Boston, Massachusetts. He is second-generation Korean American.

Mitchell Kim is lead pastor at Living Water Alliance Church in Warrenville, Illinois. He is second-generation Korean American.

Sam S. Kim is youth pastor and director of Christian education at Open Door Presbyterian Church in Herndon, Virginia. Second-generation Korean American, he is also pastor of marriage and family life for the English ministry at Open Door.

David Lee is pastor at Harvest Community Church in Hoffman Estates, Illinois. He is second-generation Korean American.

Biak Mang is pastor of Myanmar Christian Church of Metro Chicago in Illinois. He is first-generation Burmese American.

Grace Y. May is pastor of the English congregation at the Overseas Chinese Mission in New York City and adjunct assistant professor of missiology at Gordon-Conwell Theological Seminary in South Hamilton, Massachusetts. She is second-generation Chinese American.

M. Sydney Park is assistant professor of divinity at Beeson Divinity School in Birmingham, Alabama. She is second-generation Korean American.

Soong-Chan Rah is the Milton B. Engebretson Associate Professor of Church Growth and Evangelism at North Park Theological Seminary in Chicago, Illinois. He is second-generation Korean American.

Nancy Sugikawa is associate pastor of serving ministries at Lighthouse Christian Church in Bellevue, Washington. She is third-generation Japanese and fourth-generation Taiwanese American.

F. Albert "Al" Tizon is associate professor of holistic ministry at Palmer Theological Seminary of Eastern University and director of Word & Deed Network of Evangelicals for Social Action in Wynnewood, Pennsylvania. He is 1.5-generation Filippino American.

Gideon Tsang is pastor at Vox Veniae Covenant Church in Austin, Texas. He is second-generation Chinese Canadian.

Timothy Tseng is president and executive director for Institute for the Study of Asian American Christianity (ISAAC) and pastor of English ministries at Canaan Taiwanese Christian Church in San Jose, California. He is 1.9-generation Chinese American.

Jonathan Wu is executive pastor of Evergreen Baptist Church of Los Angeles in Rosemead, California. He is second-generation Chinese American.

Greg J. Yee is associate superintendent of the Pacific Southwest Conference of the Evangelical Covenant Church in Sacramento, California. He is fifth-generation Chinese American.

Peter K. Yi is pastor at Young Nak Presbyterian Church English Ministry in Toronto, Ontario, Canada. He is second-generation Korean American.